LEGO Wind Energy

Green Energy Projects with Mindstorms EV3

Grady Koch
Elias Koch

Apress®

LEGO Wind Energy: Green Energy Projects with Mindstorms EV3

Grady Koch
Yorktown, VA, USA

Elias Koch
Freiburg im Breisgau, Baden-Württemberg,
Germany

ISBN-13 (pbk): 978-1-4842-4438-8
https://doi.org/10.1007/978-1-4842-4439-5

ISBN-13 (electronic): 978-1-4842-4439-5

Library of Congress Control Number: 2019935568

Managing Director, Apress Media LLC: Welmoed Spahr
Acquisitions Editor: Aaron Black
Development Editor: James Markham
Coordinating Editor: Jessica Vakili

Cover image designed by Freepik (www.freepik.com)

Distributed to the book trade worldwide by Springer Science+Business Media New York, 233 Spring Street, 6th Floor, New York, NY 10013. Phone 1-800-SPRINGER, fax (201) 348-4505, email orders-ny@springer-sbm.com, or visit www.springeronline.com. Apress Media, LLC is a California LLC and the sole member (owner) is Springer Science + Business Media Finance Inc (SSBM Finance Inc). SSBM Finance Inc is a **Delaware** corporation.

For information on translations, please email rights@apress.com or visit http://www.apress.com/rights-permissions.

Apress titles may be purchased in bulk for academic, corporate, or promotional use. eBook versions and licenses are also available for most titles. For more information, reference our Print and eBook Bulk Sales web page at http://www.apress.com/bulk-sales.

Any source code or other supplementary material referenced by the author in this book is available to readers on GitHub via the book's product page, located at www.apress.com/978-1-4842-4438-8. For more detailed information, please visit http://www.apress.com/source-code.

Printed on acid-free paper

For Melissa

Table of Contents

About the Authors

Grady Koch emphasizes building things from LEGO that can be applied to practical use in science, engineering, or security. He is the author of *LEGO Optics: Projects in Optical and Laser Science with LEGO, High-Tech LEGO: Projects in Science, Engineering, and Spycraft with Technic and Mindstorms EV3*, and *Secrets of Eli's LEGO Collection*. He also writes for and runs hightechlego.com, which features various LEGO technology projects. His day job since 1987 has been as a research engineer with the NASA Langley Research Center. There, he works with technology for remote sensing atmospheric phenomena. He holds a PhD in electrical engineering and holds three patents in the field of wind measurements with lidar.

Elias Koch is a homeschool student whose curriculum is largely based on LEGO.

About the Technical Reviewer

Gene L. Harding is an associate professor of electrical and computer engineering technology at Purdue University, where he has taught since 2003. He has three years of industrial experience with Agilent Technologies, has 28 years of combined active and reserve service in the United States Air Force, holds an MSEE from Rose-Hulman Institute of Technology, and is a licensed professional engineer. Professor Harding coached FIRST LEGO League teams in a highly competitive region for five years while his son was participating. In his final year of coaching his team placed second in the state out of over 300 teams and qualified for the international tournament at Legoland, where his team won the Core Values Teamwork award and placed third in the Robot Game out of 72 teams from all over the world.

Introduction

Electrical power is so much the foundation of today's society that we've felt the need to produce power from scratch, even if it's only a little. We could purchase a diesel generator or solar-power array, but we find the idea unsatisfying since this would not really help us to understand or build a capability ourselves. Building a machine is to truly understand the machine—hence our fascination over the years with LEGO. LEGO makes building machines easy. And so our journey began to generate electricity from LEGO parts.

Wind has been used as a power source for millennia, perhaps because it's easy to harness with relatively simple technology. Sailboats are known to have been in use for at least 5,000 years. The earliest known use of wind energy to turn a wheel is from Heron of Alexandria in the first century A.D., who used wind to power a musical organ. In the seventh century, windmills were invented to grind grain and pump water, and such use flourished throughout the world. In 1887, the first wind turbine for generating electricity was built in Scotland by James Blyth. Today, wind power provides about 4 percent of the world's generated electricity.

Now, with this book, people can join in on the wind-energy adventure using their LEGO collection. We don't mean LEGO models that look like miniature wind turbines. This book shows functioning wind turbines that generate electricity. It's not much electricity, and if a person's interest is in micro-scale wind turbines for practical use, there are many such pre-made devices available on the market. Rather, this book is for people who want to learn how turbines work, are participating in a wind power design competition, are generally interested in alternative energy, or are LEGO fans looking for a new direction. LEGO does make a wind-power kit in set 9688 Renewable Energy Add-On, but it's a fairly simple kit that involves pressing together a few elements, including pre-made turbine blades. We found this set rather lacking for a person seeking to explore and understand how turbines work and how to optimize performance. The LEGO system's great variety offers so much more in design possibility.

One reason to look into homemade wind turbines is that many students take part in wind turbine design competitions, such as the KidWind Challenge, Collegiate Wind Competition, and locally organized contests. The use of LEGO is permissible by the rules of these competitions, but seems not to be well exploited. In this book, examples are given that fit within the KidWind Challenge, including adherence to rules of the competition, such as that a specific generator be used.

Wind turbines are perhaps so popular for educational competitions because their construction touches on many aspects of science and engineering: aerodynamics, mechanics, structures, electricity, electronics, and meteorology. There's much that can be learned by building a wind turbine, but, on the other hand, the complexity can make it difficult to know where to start. We wrote this book to give such a start, with the many aspects of the turbine addressed with practical examples. We give specific design instructions for turbine construction, but also provide suggestions and background science to go in new directions. Our hope is to encourage people to create their own designs. Considering that kids of middle-school age may be interested in this topic, we've written this book so that such kids can understand the material with the help of an adult coach. High school students can likely work through the material on their own.

LEGO parts come in a bewildering variety, so to identify parts we use a convention of part number and description. This part number can be typed into online marketplaces, such as `bricklink.com`. For example, the iconic LEGO brick would be identified as

`#3001 2x4 Brick`

Assembly diagrams are used throughout the book, made with the Studio utility from bricklink.com. Parts are identified in the assembly diagram, as well as in parts lists in the appendix. Color choice is, of course, up to the builder's taste. We tend to favor black and grey color schemes, but there is nothing wrong with choosing festive colors or even whatever color is on hand.

As when building any machinery, consideration should be given to safety. The electrical power generated by the turbine designs in this book is rather low and is not likely to present a hazard. Rather, the most hazardous aspect of this book's material is from parts coming loose and flying through the air, creating an eye hazard. We've had many instances of turbine blades breaking loose during high-speed rotation. These blades are not heavy enough to hurt, except for the possibility of eye injury. So, it's vitally important to wear safety glasses during the experiments described in this book.

CHAPTER 1

The Generator

A generator is the foundation for electrical power generation, creating electrical current from rotary-motion input. Wind provides the rotary motion for a wind turbine generator. This chapter involves experimenting with generators by working with a LEGO-based design, including the construction of a hand-cranked generator that uses manual motion to spin it. In later chapters, this manual rotation will be replaced by energy from wind.

Generator Basics

Generators create electricity by spinning a coil of wire near a magnet via the principle of electromagnetic induction. The physicist Michael Faraday studied the phenomenon of induction, quantifying it in the law that bears his name. The essence of Faraday's law is that an electromotive force is generated in the coil, and that force is related to the time rate of change of the magnet's field strength. Consideration of Faraday's law indicates that to generate higher electrical power two approaches can be taken: (1) using a strong magnet, or (2) moving the wire coil quickly. Spinning the magnet is an effective way to move the wire coil quickly.

© Grady Koch 2019
G. Koch and E. Koch, *LEGO Wind Energy*, https://doi.org/10.1007/978-1-4842-4439-5_1

To illustrate how generators are actually built, Figure 1-1 shows a LEGO-based generator with the cover removed. In the opened generator, the edge of the disk of wire coils, called a *rotor*, and the edge of the magnet can be seen. Taking apart a generator as done here is likely to damage the device and is not recommended. We sacrificed a generator in our collection in the name of scientific advancement.

Figure 1-1. *The LEGO #71427c01 motor—or generator, in this case—is shown both with and without its cover*

Further disassembly of the generator, seen in Figure 1-2, shows more of the parts involved, including the rotor/magnet core, spinning axle, steel annulus, and electrical connections. *Brushes* are fine wires that touch the commutator to connect electrical output to end use. The hole in the steel annulus goes over the commutator assembly to shape and concentrate the magnetic field created by the magnet. The *commutator* is a segmented metal ring used to periodically reverse the electrical current direction so that direct current output results, rather than alternating current. When the motor is assembled, the brushes press up against the commutator. Figure 1-3 gives a close-up view of the rotor/magnet core. The rotor is at the front of this view, featuring three coils of wire that spin about an axle that has a commutator on the end. Each coil of wire has two electrical connections; hence, there are six segments making up the commutator to accommodate all three coils. Electrical output is connected from the commutator by contact with the brushes seen in Figure 1-2. The magnet is a disk attached behind the rotor, with the magnet surface visible through the holes of the rotor's wire coils.

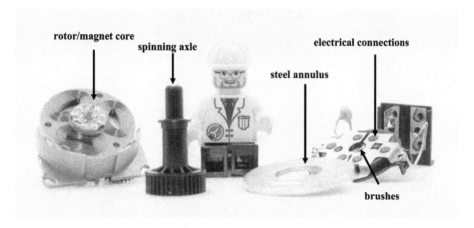

Figure 1-2. *Taking apart the pieces of the #71427c01 device shows the rotor/magnet core, spinning axle, steel annulus, and electrical connections*

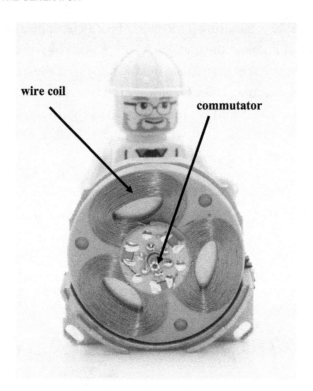

Figure 1-3. *A close-up view of the rotor/magnet core shows the wire coils, commutator, and magnet*

The generator shown in Figure 1-1 was not intended to be used as a generator—it's actually a motor. But motors and generators are closely related, being sort of inverses of each other. Motors create rotary motion with an electrical input, whereas a generator uses rotary motion to create electrical output. By grabbing the shaft of a motor and spinning it, an electrical current will be generated at the motor's electrical contacts. LEGO has never made a generator, but has made many types of motors. Several such LEGO motors produced over the years are shown in Figure 1-4. Only a few types of LEGO motors are suitable to be used as a generator, since most have gear systems built into their housings to make them more suitable for building vehicles or robots. This gearing can involve too high a torque for turning the rotor shaft. Furthermore, some LEGO motor designs have complicated connections to accommodate encoders for precision control, as used in the Mindstorms EV3 and Power Functions motors. LEGO's older and simpler designs work best as a generator, such as the #71427c01 Electric Technic Mini-Motor 9V and the #2838c01 Electric Technic Motor 9V. The best-performing generator found after trying all of the devices shown in Figure 1-4 is #71427c01, also featured in Figures 1-1 to 1-3. Second best is the #2838c01. Third best is the #87577c01 Power Functions E Motor, giving an option if a modern motor is desired. The #2838c01 and #71427c01 motors have been out of production for several years but can readily be found on bricklink.com. The #71427c01 motor has a cousin in #43362c01, with an almost identical case, but different internal construction. #71427c01 and #43362c01 can be distinguished from each other by weight, as #71427c01 is heavier.

Figure 1-4. *LEGO motors to consider for use as a generator include: (1) #71427c01 Technic Mini-Motor 9V, (2) #58120c01 Power Functions M Motor, (3) #87577c01 Power Functions E Motor, (4) #99455 EV3 Medium Servo Motor, and (5) #2838c01 9V Motor*

Putting a Generator to Use

A generator can be used to build a simple hand-crank flashlight, as shown in Figure 1-5 and in video at hightechlego.com. Step-by-step directions to build the flashlight are given here. Cranking the handle turns the generator enough to light up the #4771 Electric Light Brick that is attached to the generator's electrical output, although the light is not very bright in this design. A gear system is obviously needed here to increase the rotation speed of the generator's shaft, the subject of the following chapter. And, of course, the end goal of this book is to have wind energy spin the crank shaft.

Figure 1-5. *A hand crank–powered flashlight can be built from a LEGO generator by following the steps shown below*

While experimentation is encouraged and is the point of this book, it's important to note that an LED (light emitting diode) shouldn't be used with the hand-crank flashlight since the generator can produce either a positive or negative voltage depending on the direction of the crank-shaft spin. A negative voltage can damage an LED, whereas the old-fashioned filament lightbulbs of the #4771 Electric Light Brick can work with either a positive or a negative voltage. An interesting feature of the #4771 is that it creates a constant light for one voltage polarity and a flashing light for the opposite voltage polarity.

7

1

2

3

4

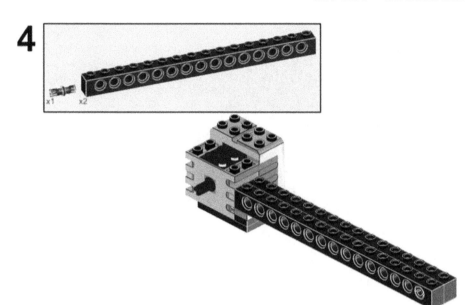

5

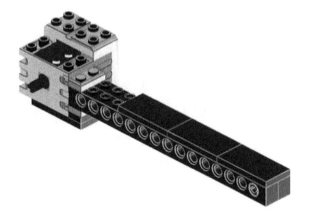

6

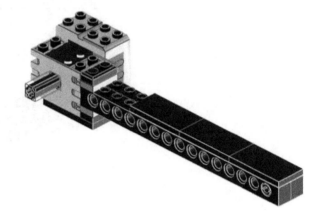

7

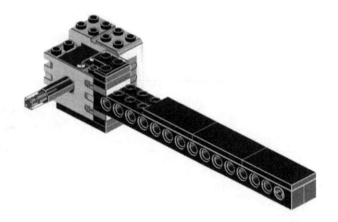

8

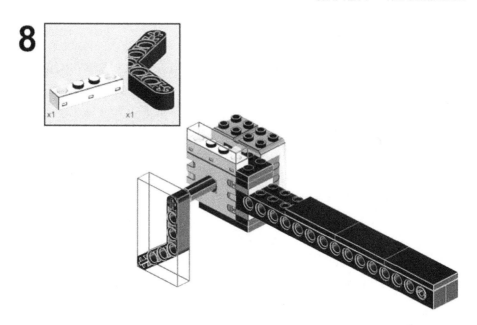

9

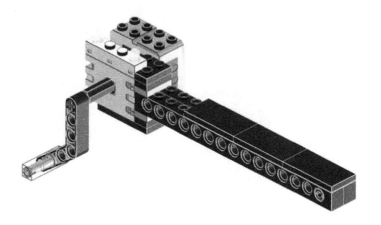

Non-LEGO Generators

A LEGO-based generator has the appeal of fitting with the LEGO system, providing convenience and options for building the rest of a turbine. For example, attaching gears to a LEGO generator is a simple task. However, a situation may arise where a different type of generator needs to be used. A prime example of this is participating in wind power design competitions, such as the KidWind Challenge, for which there is a rule that a specific generator must be used, such as the one shown in Figure 1-6, purchased from Vernier Software and Technology (vernier.com). The KidWind-approved generator is shown in Figure 1-6, along with LEGO part additions. With this added LEGO compatibility, the rest of the turbine construction can proceed with LEGO elements.

Figure 1-6. *A generator specified for the KidWind Challenge has LEGO parts added so that it can be used with the LEGO system*

Modifications to the KidWind generator include (1) a #32065 1x7 Thin Technic Liftarm for mounting, and (2) the attachment on the generator shaft of an adapter to a LEGO-compatible axle. The 1x7 Thin Technic Liftarm requires enlargement of the center hole to fit over the center of the generator, as shown in Figure 1-7, with this enlargement achieved by a tapered reamer tool. The reamer is turned into the center hole of the liftarm a little at a time, alternating sides of the hole as it progresses. Frequent fit checks are done as the liftarm hole is gradually enlarged. When the liftarm hole is just large enough to fit over the generator, it is permanently fixed into place with five-minute epoxy. The shaft/axle adapter takes advantage of a part made for a product line of motors called Pololu, available at robotshop.com (Product Code: RB-Pol-137) or at hightechlego.com. This Pololu adapter fits with the KidWind generator after a minor procedure to slightly enlarge the spindle mounting hole, as shown in Figure 1-8. Enlargement involves turning a 5/64 drill bit into the opening of the shaft. The bit should be turned by hand, not with a motorized drill. Pliers or vice grips can be used if more leverage is needed to turn the drill bit. After enlargement, a speck of cyanoacrylate glue (Super Glue or Krazy Glue) applied before inserting over the KidWind generator ensures the adapter stays in place.

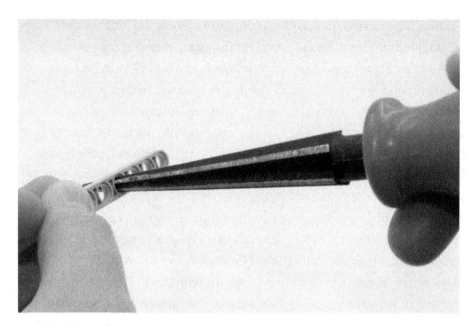

Figure 1-7. *The center hole of a #32065 1x7 Technic Liftarm needs a little enlargement to fit over a collar on the KidWind generator*

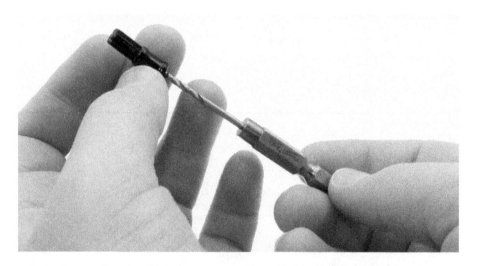

Figure 1-8. *The shaft diameter on the Pololu shaft/axle adapter needs a little enlargement to fit over the shaft of the KidWind generator*

14

Generator Wire Connections

Connecting to a KidWind generator is simple because the generator is sold with two wires already attached. These two wires are connected to a measurement device during the KidWind competition. LEGO generators have different styles of cables, depending on the type of generator. Referring to Figure 1-4, the older devices of #71427c01 and #2838c01 use the #5306 Wire Cable. The newer Power Functions generators, #58120c01 and #87577c01, have power cables attached to them, which can be extended using the Power Functions #60656 Extension Wire. Both the #60656 and #5306 cables are shown in Figure 1-9. Connecting to the #60656 and #5306 for turbine power output can be done with alligator clips, as will be described in Chapter 6. The #60656 is dual use in that it can accommodate the older #2838c01 and #58120c01 generators, as well as the Power Functions devices. This backward compatibility is useful since the #5306 Wire Cable is getting harder to find in new condition. Connecting to the EV3 motor requires a breakout connector that gets a bit complicated—examples are shown at hightechlego.com.

Figure 1-9. *The connectors on two LEGO wire cables are on the #5306 Wire Cable (left) and the Power Functions #60656 Extension Wire (right)*

Summary

This chapter has presented how generators use the principle of electromagnetic induction to produce electricity. The LEGO implementation of a generator was shown, adapting LEGO-intended designs for motors as generators. LEGO has made many types of motors over the years, some performing better than others as generators. Our experiments showed that the #71427c01 Technic Mini-Motor worked the best as a generator in terms of highest power output. Some instances, such as a wind turbine design competition, may call for a non-LEGO generator to be used. For such a case, designs were shown to make a non-LEGO generator compatible with the LEGO system so the rest of the wind turbine can be built from LEGO. This chapter closed with an explanation of electrical cable connections to various LEGO generators. In the next chapter, gearbox designs will be described to allow for a higher rotation speed in a generator.

CHAPTER 2

The Gearbox

A gearbox is used in wind turbines to increase the rotation speed given to the generator shaft and involves two or more gears that increase the speed from the rotational input. This increased rotation speed makes the wind turbine produce a higher electrical output power. Gearbox design involves some complexity in choosing gears as rotation speed and torque must both be managed. The interplay between torque and speed is demonstrated in this chapter by building upon the hand-crank generator of Chapter 1.

LEGO Gears

The gearbox of a wind turbine converts the relatively low speed of a spinning shaft to the higher speed needed to drive a generator. The hand-crank flashlight in Chapter 1 showed that a slowly spinning shaft is rather inefficient at driving a generator. Increasing the speed of rotation can be accomplished with gears. A fundamental principle of gear systems helps in understanding the design process: speed and torque are involved in a trade-off compromise. In other words, speed comes at the expense of torque and vice versa. Torque is the amount of rotational energy involved in a rolling or spinning machine. When a rolling machine, such as a car, is at a standstill a high torque is needed to get the car under way, so a high-torque gear arrangement is used. But this gear arrangement won't get the car moving very fast. Hence, once the car is moving, a different gear arrangement is engaged for lower torque and higher speed. Selecting various gear ratios is the function of a transmission.

© Grady Koch 2019
G. Koch and E. Koch, *LEGO Wind Energy*, https://doi.org/10.1007/978-1-4842-4439-5_2

LEGO gears offer a wonderfully convenient means to explore the workings of gears. A sampling of gears relevant for the construction of a wind turbine is pictured in Figure 2-1. A gear is described by how many teeth it has—a smaller diameter gear has fewer teeth. The grey gears on the right side of Figure 2-1 are an older design that is common among Technic sets, with 8, 24, and 40 teeth. We tend to favor these older gears for a wind turbine because their narrow widths present a little less friction and because they offer a high gear-ratio possibility from two gears; the 40-tooth and 8-tooth gear combination gives a gear ratio of 5. The black gears on the left side of Figure 2-1 are useful in some applications involving high torque where thick, strong gears are desirable. The thick gears also feature bevels on the sides of the teeth, so the gears can be mated perpendicular to each other as well as the typical in-line arrangement.

Figure 2-1. *Gears useful for wind-turbine construction include: (1) black, at left, double-bevel gears of Mindstorms EV3 in 12, 20, and 36 teeth, and (2) grey, at right, older Technic gears in 8, 24, and 40 teeth*

Gearing Up

Increasing the speed of rotation, as is needed to use a turbine shaft to drive a generator shaft, can be accomplished by using a big gear to drive a small gear. Figure 2-2 shows such a design, with a 40-tooth gear driving a 24-tooth gear in the hand-crank generator from Chapter 1. Step-by-step building instructions follow Figure 2-2. The increase in rotation speed from this gear arrangement can be found by the ratio of gear teeth:

```
speed increase = 40/24 = 1.7
```

This improves the performance and brightness of the flashlight over the case of using no gears, seen in Chapter 1. But associated with the speed increase is a need to increase the torque applied to the crank handle.

Figure 2-2. *A 40-to-24 gearing added to the hand-crank generator from Chapter 1 gives the generator a higher rotation speed*

1

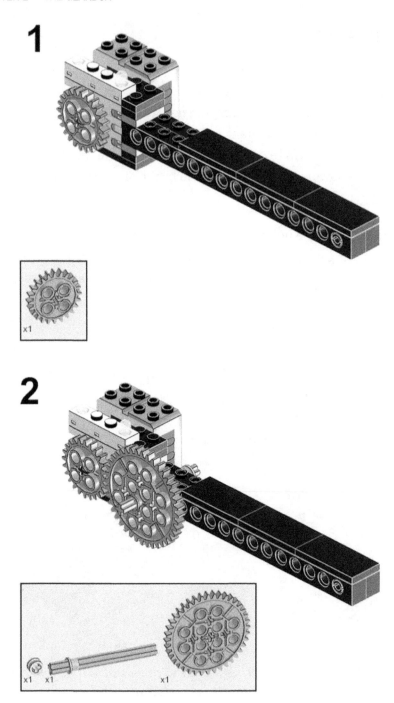

2

3

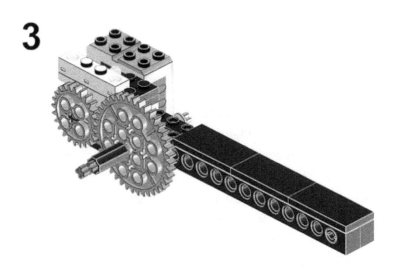

4

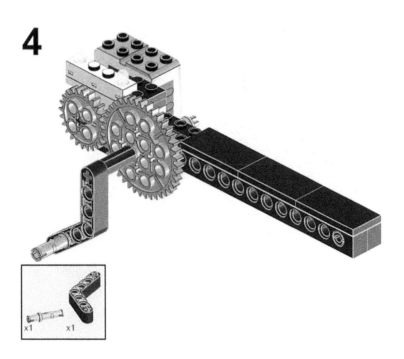

Increasing the gear ratio further, as pictured in Figure 2-3, a 40-tooth gear driving an 8-tooth gear really steps up the brightness of the flashlight. Steps for building this higher-speed version of the hand-crank generator are the same as for Figure 2-2, but with the use of a different pair of holes in the 1x16 Technic Brick with Holes so as to accommodate the new gear pairing. While this provides higher-speed rotation, the torque required to turn the crank handle is so high that the axle holding the 40-tooth gear flexes and bends. This gear ratio of 5 pushes the limit of torque that the LEGO assembly can handle, and a similar consideration is involved for the design of a turbine. In building a wind turbine, a design consideration is the gear ratio to use. A higher gear ratio is desirable in order to rapidly spin the generator input. However, at too high a gear ratio the required input torque may be so high that the turbine's rotor won't spin because there is too much resistance to overcome before rotation can start.

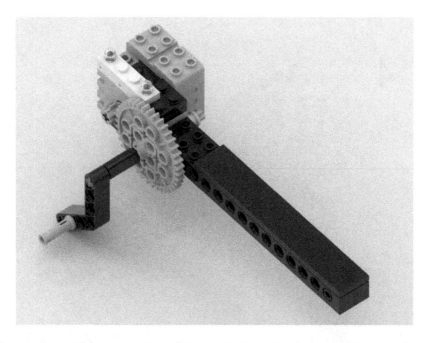

Figure 2-3. *The gear ratio of Figure 2-2 can be increased to a value of 5 by having a 40-tooth gear drive an 8-tooth gear*

Compound Gears

More than two gears can be used to tailor a gear ratio. Sets of gears can be arranged in a design of compound gears, which involves two gears placed on either side of an axle. As shown in Figure 2-4 and the construction instructions that follow, each of these two gears in turn meshes with other gears. The speed increase in a compound gear system is the product of the gear-ratio pairs. For example, for the design of Figure 2-4:

```
speed increase = 40/24 x 40/24 = 2.8
```

Compound gear designs allow for a wider range of gear ratios over a single pair of gears. Also, compound gears extend the length over which the rotation takes place, which is useful in cases where a longer distance is needed for the positions of the rotating shafts.

Figure 2-4. *The hand-crank generator from Figure 2-2 has been modified with a compound gear design involving a 40-tooth gear and a 24-tooth gear on the same axle*

1

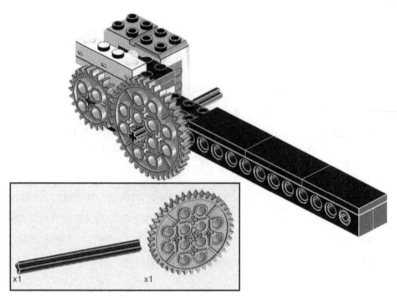

2

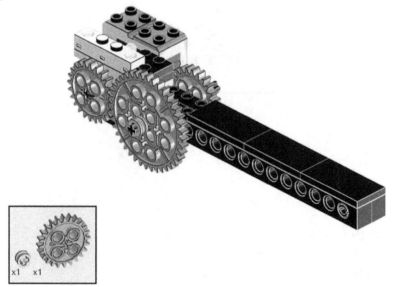

3

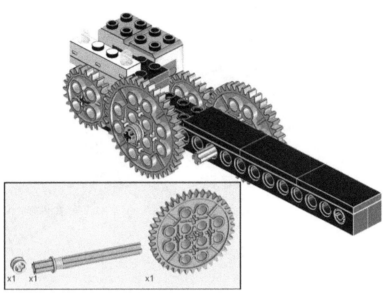

4

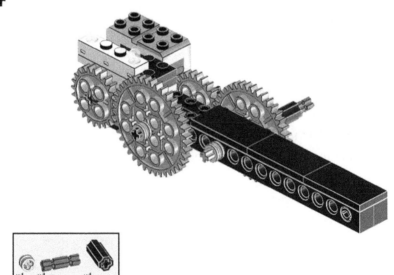

5

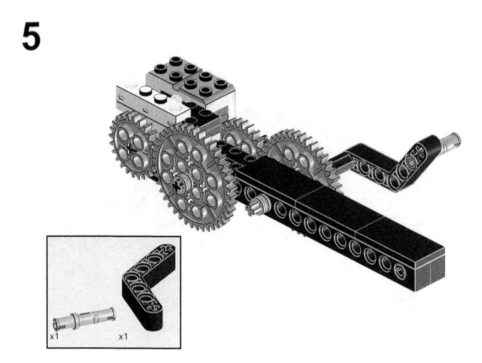

Summary

Gear designs have been presented in this chapter to provide options for finding the best gear ratio. Compound gears allow for the fine-tuning of the gear ratio or for very high gear ratios. However, every gear added to a system contributes to energy loss by friction. So, compound gears can build up losses in the efficiency of power generation. With the goal of achieving the highest efficiency in mind, our experiments found that a simple two-gear system works better than a compound gear design. But we also found that a gear ratio higher than 5, which is the maximum that can be achieved using two Technic gears, might be desired. An option for a large-diameter gear is found in the custom 3D-printing marketplace, with an example we found on shapeways.com shown in Figure 2-5. This 56-tooth gear offers a gear ratio of 7 when partnered with an 8-tooth gear.

Choosing the most effective gear design is hard to accomplish until a complete turbine is built. Some trial and error may be involved once the turbine is fully built, so it's convenient to mount the generator such that various gear ratios can be tried. Such mounts are shown in the following chapters.

Figure 2-5. *A custom 3D-printed gear with 56 teeth provides an option beyond the largest gear that LEGO produces, which has 40 teeth*

CHAPTER 3

The Vertical-Axis Turbine

Wind-turbine designs can be classified as either vertical axis or horizontal axis, referring to the axis about which the rotor spins. Most turbines seen in use are horizontal axis, as that style is more efficient than vertical axis turbines. This difference in efficiency is largely a matter of aerodynamics—horizontal-axis turbines' blades take full advantage of aerodynamic lift. Vertical-axis turbines are easier to build, though, offering some advantages in their simpler design. For example, vertical-axis turbines need no consideration of pointing into the wind, as they use wind from any direction to spin.

Catching the Wind

Figure 3-1 shows a LEGO vertical-axis turbine that uses cups to catch the wind and spin a rotor shaft. These cups are 11x11 Cylinder Hemispheres arranged 120 degrees apart from each other. We used 11x11 Cylinder Hemispheres from the Star Wars theme (such as #98107pb04 of the planet Kamino) for an interesting look. But plain cylinders can be found, such as #98107. Multiple triads of cups can be stacked to catch more wind, such as the three stacks in Figure 3-1. Different directions of rotation, either clockwise or counterclockwise, can be achieved based on the direction the cups face—the turbine in Figure 3-1 uses clockwise rotation. This direction of travel can make a difference in generator output power, with some generators favoring a direction of rotation. Construction of this example turbine is broken down into several assemblies, described in the following sections.

Figure 3-1. *The vertical-axis turbine gets its name from the axis about which rotation occurs*

Generator Mount

A mount to hold a generator for a vertical-axis wind turbine is shown in Figure 3-2; building instructions follow the figure. This mount is based on the #71427c01 generator, though similar structures could be built for any of the LEGO generators discussed in Chapter 1 and pictured in Figure 1-4. A key feature of this mount is the accommodation of a vertical shaft, to which the turbine rotor will later be attached. In other words, the generator is facing upward. Another structure, to be built later in this chapter, will fit on top of the generator mount to hold a gearbox.

Figure 3-2. *A structure is built to hold a #71427c01 generator firmly in place with an axle connector pointed vertically*

1

2

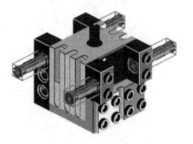

3

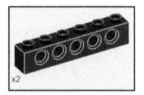

x2

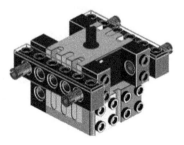

4

x2

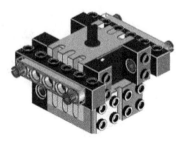

5

x2

6

x2

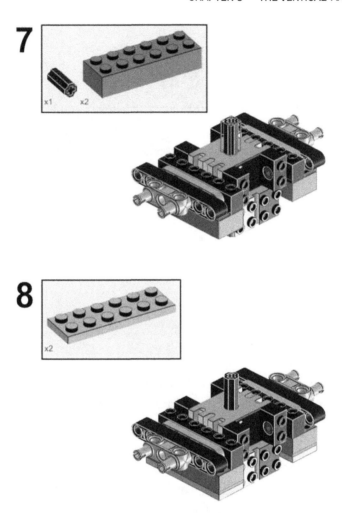

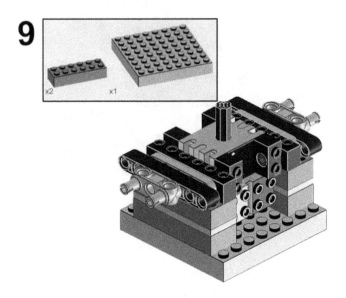

Gearbox Frame

Figure 3-3 shows a frame to hold the gears for the gearbox, as well as to provide mounting holes for the spinning turbine shaft. Step-by-step instructions for building the frame are given following Figure 3-3. The rotor shaft is not yet shown, as it will be inserted in a step later in the chapter. The shaft with gear that does appear in the figure transfers rotation from the rotor to the generator, with a gear that can be changed depending on the desired gear ratio. A 24-tooth gear is seen in Figure 3-3, but this could be replaced with any other desired gear size. The rotor shaft will also have a gear placed on it, with the shaft placed in the hole in the red 1x13 Liftarm that allows mating to the generator shaft gear. Both shafts are held at two places in this design—at the top by a red #32525 1x11 Liftarm and at the bottom by a black #41239 1x13 Liftarm.

Figure 3-3. *The generator frame is based on an open center frame and Technic liftarms*

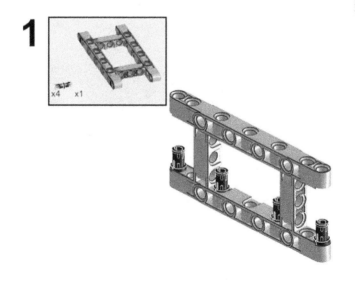

2

3

4

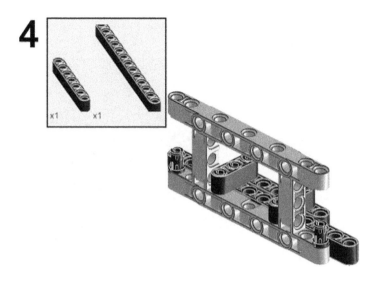

5

6

7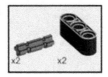

8

9

10

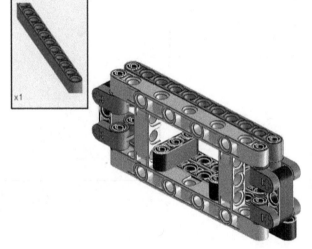

11

12

13

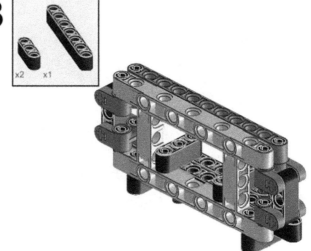

14

15

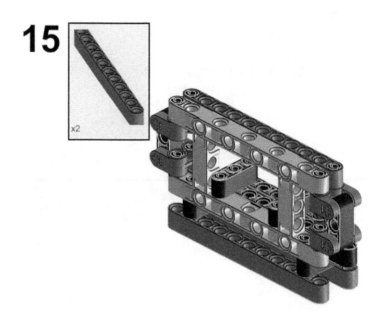

16

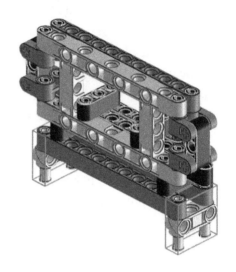

17

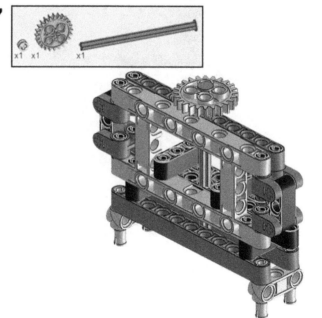

Joining the Generator and Gearbox

The generator mount (Figure 3-2) and gearbox frame (Figure 3-3) snap together as shown in Figure 3-4, and the geared axle of the top section engages with the #6538c Technic Axle Connector of the bottom section. Also installed here is a #5306 cable for the generator, which will be hooked up to an electrical load in Chapters 6 and 8. The generator and gearbox ride on top of a pedestal. A high platform is desirable since wind very close to the ground is diminished in speed. But the platform shouldn't be so tall as to become top heavy and fall over. An example pedestal platform is seen in Figure 3-1, with the assembled generator/gearbox attached to a tower 40 centimeters tall. The pedestal has a square cross section and is wider near the bottom to give stability to the tower.

Figure 3-4. *The gearbox fits on top of the generator, and the assembled structure then mounts to the top of a pedestal as seen in Figure 3-1*

The Rotor

The rotor is based on cups that catch the wind to spin a shaft. A large surface area is needed for a cup, and various LEGO plates and disks are possible solutions. We found that 11x11 Cylinder Hemispheres serve particularly well as turbine cups, with curved shapes that effectively catch the wind. Three such cups are arranged 120 degrees apart from each other such that the wind direction is always being caught by a cup. The next cup in line then spins into position to be pushed by the wind. The 120-degree spacing of the cups is set by using a #57585 Technic Axle Connector Hub as a center point. The center of this hub also serves as an axle connection point.

Sets of cups can be stacked to catch more wind—the design of Figure 3-1 has three stacks. But consideration has to be given to the extra rotation allowed by a set of cups versus the loss of rotational energy that results from the weight and friction of the cups. The design for each rotor is the same, as shown in Figure 3-5; assembly directions follow the figure.

Figure 3-5. *The vertical-axis rotor is based on a #57585 Technic Axle Connector Hub*

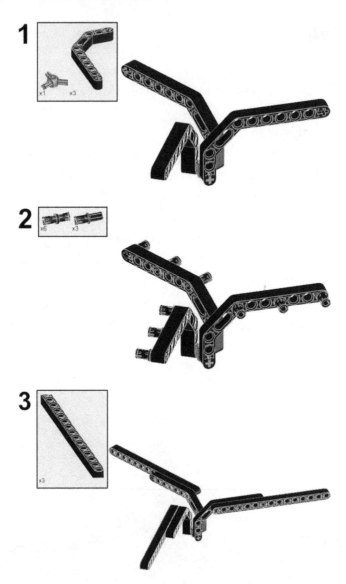

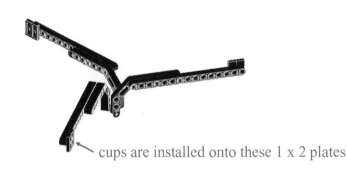

cups are installed onto these 1 x 2 plates

Final Assembly

To finish the turbine, a long axle is placed through the center hole of one or more rotors. A gear is slid up onto the axle, then backed with a bushing. As shown in Figure 3-6, the rotor axle is placed into a hole on the liftarm to mate with the gear that turns the generator. The rotor axle that sticks into the gearbox frame should be long enough for the axle to be held in two places: (1) on the top of the gearbox frame, and (2) lower down, partway through a hole of the 1x13 Liftarm (placed in Step 4 of the gearbox frame construction). In Figure 3-6, a 1:1 gear ratio is used, but changing the gear ratio is a simple matter of sliding on different-sized gears.

For higher rotation speed, multiple triads of rotors can be stacked onto the main rotor axle. In Figures 3-1 and 3-6 three rotors are stacked, with the first and third triads in the stack oriented on the rotor axle so they are aligned with each other. The second rotor in the stack is aligned to be between the first and third. In experimenting with multiple rotor stacks, we found that the central axle was flexing a lot after a two-rotor stack. To eliminate this flexing we used an axle made of stainless steel that can be found at the bricklink.com store of Brick Machine Shop. Various lengths are available for these custom parts, as shown in Figure 3-7.

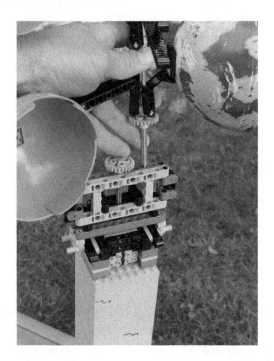

Figure 3-6. *Final assembly includes inserting an axle through the center hole of each rotor set*

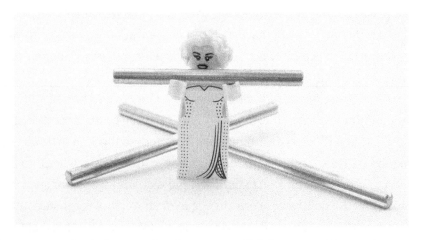

Figure 3-7. *Stainless steel axles are available as an alternative to standard plastic LEGO axles, coming in handy when standard plastic LEGO axles flex too much*

Mount for KidWind Generator

The assembly shown in Figure 3-6 and developed earlier in this chapter is based on a LEGO generator, but a KidWind generator can also be used. The KidWind generator was presented in Chapter 1 in case a non-LEGO generator is called for. The use of the KidWind generator is shown in Figure 3-8, assuming the KidWind generator has been modified with LEGO connections as was done in Figure 1-6. To hold the KidWind generator for a vertical-axis wind turbine, the same gearbox frame developed earlier in this chapter can be used. The needed change involves just the generator mount. As shown in the assembly diagrams following Figure 3-8, the KidWind generator mount is based on #64179 5x7 Open Center Frames.

Figure 3-8. *The same gearbox from Figure 3-3 can be used with the KidWind generator*

51

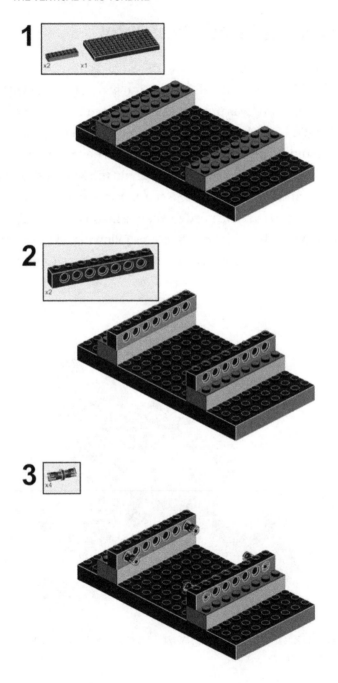

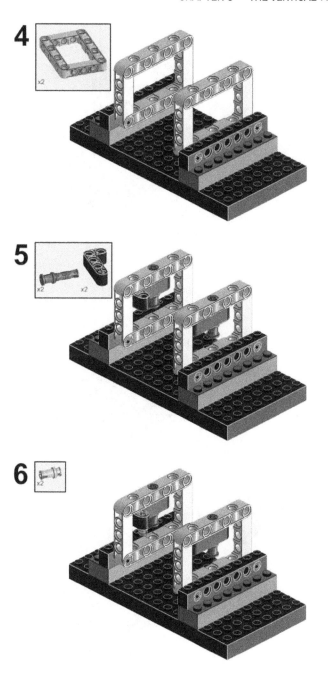

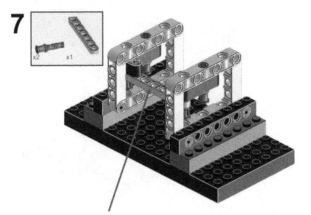

1 x 7 Thin Liftarm is part of KidWind generator mount of Figure 1-6.

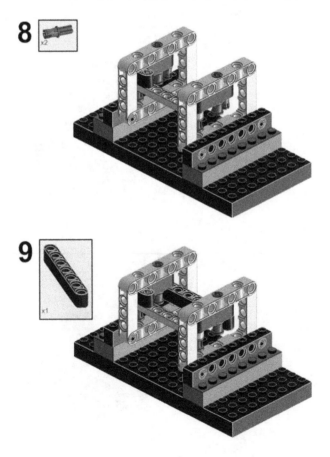

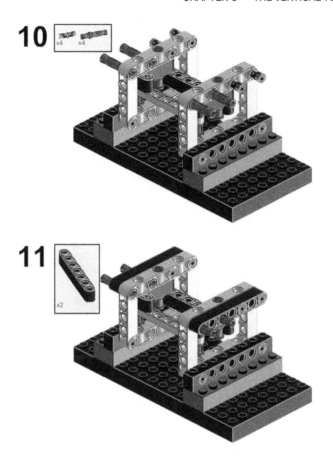

Summary

This chapter presented a complete wind turbine that uses aerodynamic drag to push a rotor into motion. The rotor spins about a vertical axis; hence, the name of this type of wind turbine. Subassemblies were built for a generator mount, gearbox frame, and rotor. Multiple rotors can be stacked on the same axis to increase the turbine's power output. An alternate generator mount was also described if a non-LEGO generator is to be used. In the next chapter, the use of aerodynamic principles is introduced to build a turbine that is more efficient than the vertical-axis implementation.

CHAPTER 4

Airfoil Blades

The cup-shaped rotors on the vertical-axis turbine of the previous chapter are a simple design to capture wind. The cups are pushed around in a circle by the wind. A much more effective way to catch the wind is to take advantage of aerodynamic principles, resulting in a capability for much higher rotation speed. The key aerodynamic principle to consider is the airfoil.

The Airfoil

An airfoil is diagrammed in Figure 4-1; it is a blade shape that uses wind flow to push a turbine blade. Airfoils work by Bernoulli's Principle, which states that air pressure is lower for faster-moving air. By inserting a blade shape of a certain design into wind flow, air can be made to flow faster over the top of the blade than under the blade. By Bernoulli's Principle, a force results that tends to push upward on the blade. If several blades are attached to a central pivot, then the blades will move in a circular pattern. Tilting the airfoil is a common arrangement, with the angle of tilt called *pitch* or *angle of attack*.

© Grady Koch 2019

G. Koch and E. Koch, *LEGO Wind Energy*, https://doi.org/10.1007/978-1-4842-4439-5_4

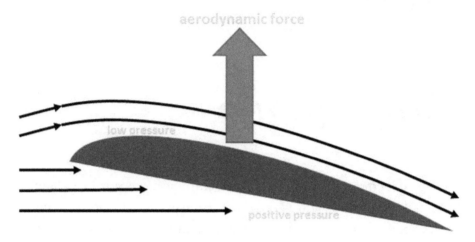

Figure 4-1. *The airfoil shape forces air to move faster over the top of the blade than under the blade*

The blades of commercial wind turbines are made by molding fiberglass into airfoil shapes, usually with sophisticated twists in the blade that improve efficiency even more. We wanted, though, to make our own blades from LEGO and explore various designs for airfoil shapes. Inspiration for how to begin with LEGO turbine blades can be taken from how airplane wings are made; airplane wings and turbine blades both use aerodynamic airfoils. Airplane wings are made by shaping the airfoil with ribs along the length of the wing, then bending sheets of aluminum over the ribs. In the LEGO approach, airfoil-shaped ribs can be built from various curved LEGO pieces, which are then wrapped with duct tape to form the blade surface. Duct tape is rather lightweight, providing an advantage in turbine-blade design, given the desire to keep the blades as light as possible. Several LEGO wind-turbine blades made this way are shown in Figure 4-2. Duct tape comes in a wide variety of textures, colors, and patterns, a few of which are shown in Figure 4-2: transparent blue, holographic, and transparent clear. The transparent tape allows the LEGO ribs to be seen underneath the tape.

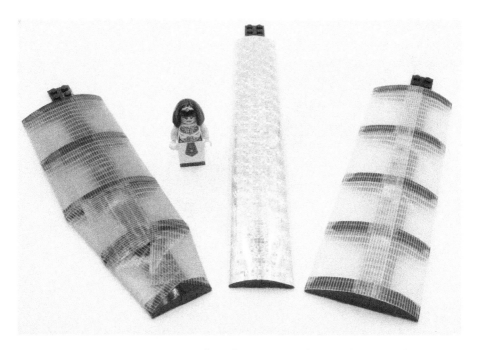

Figure 4-2. *We experimented with many airfoil and blade shapes, with only a few shown here*

Construction of these blades begins with the LEGO rib skeleton, such as that shown in Figure 4-3 and construction steps that follow. Several such blades are needed for the turbine, with experimentation warranted to find the optimum number of blades. Our research found that three blades performed best. The rib skeleton has a tab of 2x3 stud dimension for attachment of the blade to the rotor, which will be described in the following chapter. The direction of turbine rotor rotation should be considered at this phase of construction, since the placement of ribs can favor either clockwise or counterclockwise blade rotation. In the example in Figure 4-3, the airfoil shape is meant for counterclockwise rotation. For clockwise rotation, the 1x3 and 1x4 curves could be reversed, as was done for the blade in Figure 4-2 wrapped in clear transparent tape.

Figure 4-3. *The airfoil shape is attached to a two-stud-wide plate at several points along the length of the blade*

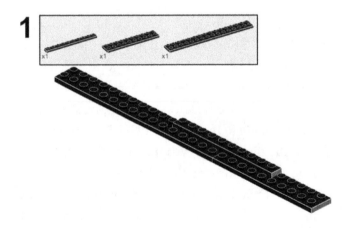

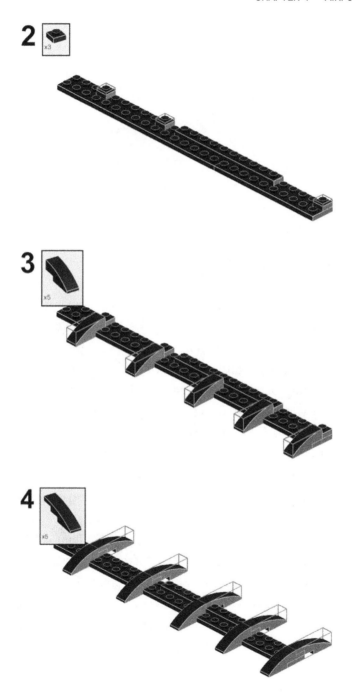

5

Wrapping in Duct Tape

Duct tape is wrapped over the ribs of the LEGO skeleton to form the surface of the turbine blade. Duct tape can be difficult to cut and shape precisely, but a couple tools can help. As shown in Figure 4-4, tools to consider are a hobby knife and scissors with non-stick coating. There are even scissors made specifically for cutting duct tape. Ordinary scissors don't work very well because the cutting edges quickly get gummed up with tape residue. The hobby knife offers more precision in cutting but can be hazardous to use. Scissors are the better choice if working with kids. Cutting tape involves not just sectioning off lengths of tape, but also trimming around corners and edges after a long section of tape has been put in place.

Taping along the length of the blade, as shown in Figure 4-5, keeps the tape taut for a good aerodynamic shape. The tape can be laid out flat, with the sticky side up, and the bottom of the blade pressed down onto the tape. Multiple layers of tape, as seen in progress in Figure 4-6, are then applied to completely cover the blade. Excess tape material is best trimmed away for each layer before moving on to the next layer.

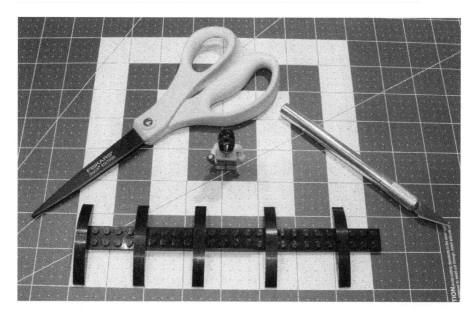

Figure 4-4. *Cutting duct tape is made simpler with tools such as scissors made with non-stick cutting edges, a hobby knife, and a cutting mat*

Figure 4-5. *A good starting point is to lay a strip of tape with the sticky side up, then press the bottom of the blade against the tape*

Figure 4-6. *The next layer of tape overlaps the first strip and is then folded over the top of the blade*

Design Ideas

The turbine blade built in Figures 4-3 and 4-4 is just one idea. Different airfoil shapes are possible using the same basic technique—a few other ideas are shown in Figure 4-7. Different blade lengths are also possible depending on your choice of the two-stud-wide plates that form the backbone of the airfoils. Figure 4-3 features a 26-stud-long backbone, but this can be changed. We tried many different lengths of blades and were surprised to find that turbine performance was best with a relatively short blade length.

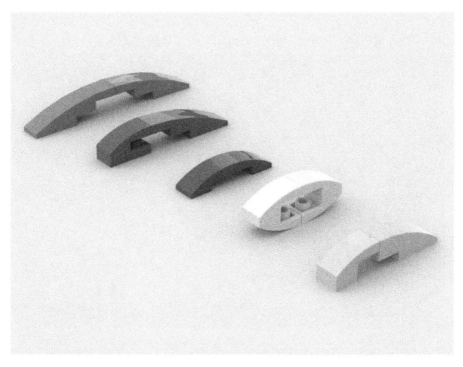

Figure 4-7. *LEGO's variety of sloped pieces offers many possible airfoil designs*

Summary

An airfoil can serve as an effective wind-turbine blade by using aerodynamic lift to provide the force to push the blade. A key feature of an airfoil is the cross-sectional shape of the blade that causes air to move faster over the top of the blade than under the blade. An airfoil shape can be built using various curved LEGO pieces distributed along a length of LEGO plate. Duct tape can then be stretched over this LEGO rib to form a turbine blade. In the following chapter, a set of airfoil blades will be used to build a horizontal-axis wind turbine.

CHAPTER 5

The Horizontal-Axis Turbine

The airfoil blades built in the previous chapter are the basis for the horizontal-axis turbine A horizontal-axis turbine produces much more electrical power than a vertical-axis design does because the blades catch a much larger area of wind. This area of capture is called the *swept area* and is defined by the diameter encircled by the airfoil blades as they spin. For comparison, the swept area of the vertical-axis turbine is the diameter of one cup of the spinning rotor, or three cups in the three-layer stack shown in Figure 4-1. The larger swept area of a horizontal-axis turbine results in a higher power-generation ability than a vertical-axis turbine. Figure 5-1 shows a completed horizontal-axis turbine consisting of the blades from Figure 4-3, a generator mount, a rotor, and a pillar. The pillar is the same tower design used for the vertical-axis turbine.

© Grady Koch 2019
G. Koch and E. Koch, *LEGO Wind Energy*, https://doi.org/10.1007/978-1-4842-4439-5_5

Figure 5-1. *The horizontal-axis turbine consists of blades, rotor, and generator/gearbox, which will be described in detail in this chapter*

The Generator/Gearbox

Figure 5-2 shows a mount for the combined generator and gearbox, and step-by-step instructions are given following the figure. The generator used as an example here is the #71427c01, but a similar design could be done for any LEGO generator. The generator and gearbox are built into the same platform for a compact size. Gears are held within the holes of a #3702 1x8 Technic Brick, such that various gear combinations can be used.

Figure 5-2 has a 40:24 gear combination, but other gear ratios could be accommodated, such as 40:8 or 24:24. A long axle sticks through one gear where the rotor will be attached, as described later in this chapter.

Figure 5-2. *The generator and gearbox are attached to an 8x8 Brick platform*

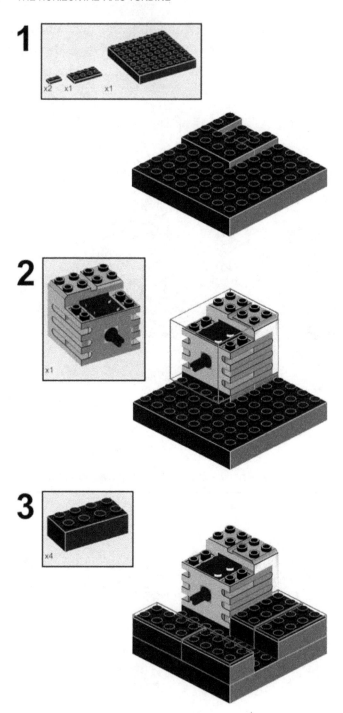

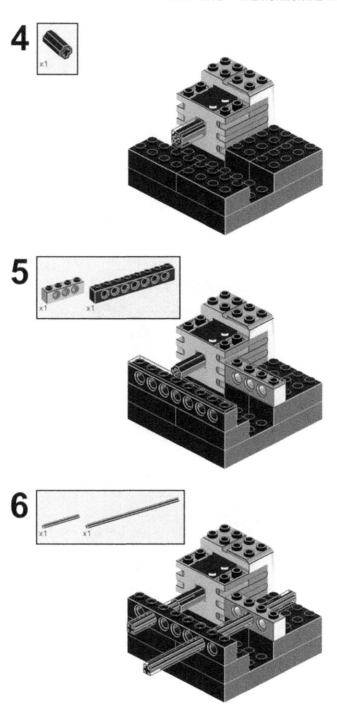

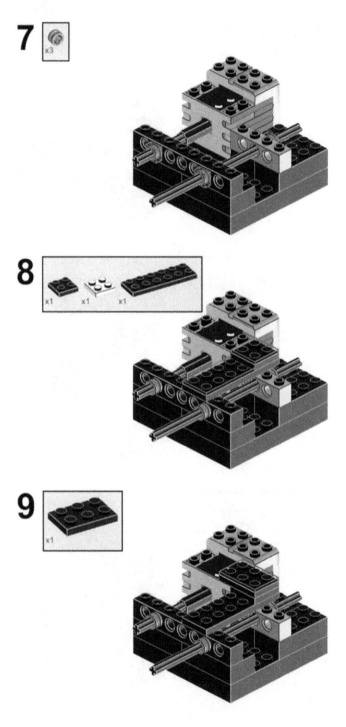

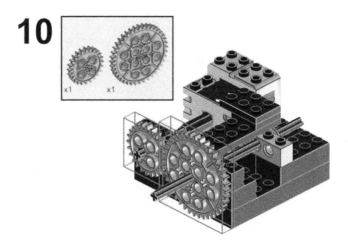

Rotor and Blade Attachment

A rotor (shown in Figure 5-3, with building instructions following the figure) provides attachment points for the blades. This rotor is similar to the vertical-axis rotor design of Chapter 3 in that it starts with a #57585 Technic Axle Connector Hub that provides connection points for bent liftarms, resulting in a three-blade design. We tried various numbers of blades from different rotor-hub attachments, but the three-blade arrangement resulted in the highest efficiency. A key feature of the rotor design is a means to vary the pitch of the blade by attachment of the blades to a hinged joint. The hinged joint is built from a #44301 and #44302 hinge plate set, giving locked angle positions to select different blade pitches of 0, 22.5, 45, and 67.5 degrees. Zero degrees, which is the angle setting in Figure 5-3, has the flat part of the blade oriented horizontally. The lock on the angle is strong enough to maintain blade pitch even when the rotor is spinning quickly.

Figure 5-3. *The rotor includes 2x2 plate attachment points for blades*

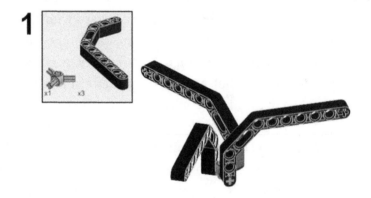

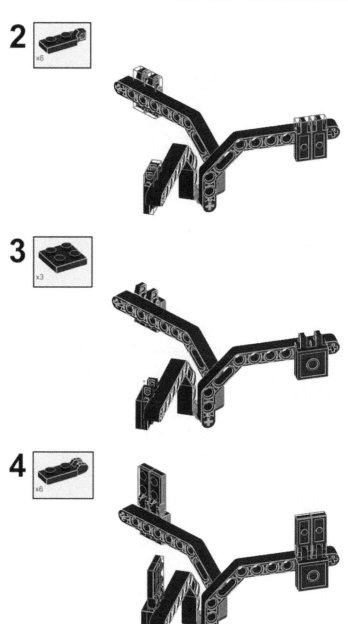

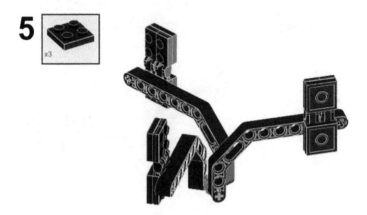

Final Assembly

The rotor slides onto the shaft of the gearbox, as shown in Figure 5-4. The blade locations shown in Figure 5-4 are set up for counterclockwise rotation of the rotor. If a clockwise rotation is desired then the locking hinges would go on the opposite side of the liftarm. Blades have also been installed in Figure 5-4, with the end of each blade mated to the 2x2 area of the locking hinge. Care should be taken that the hinge angles are all the same for the blades before proceeding to the test of Chapter 6; otherwise, the rotor will have a lopsided spin.

Figure 5-4. *The rotor slides onto the axle of the gearbox*

Mount for KidWind Generator

If a non-LEGO generator is going to be used, see the example given in Figure 5-5 of a mount for the KidWind generator. Step-by-step assembly instructions follow Figure 5-5. The KidWind generator is assumed in this construction to have been modified with LEGO adapters, as in Figure 1-6. A 40:8 gearbox is used in the example in Figure 5-5, but the gears can be changed by using different holes in the #41239 1x13 Liftarm.

Figure 5-5. *The mount for the KidWind generator makes use of the LEGO parts epoxied onto the generator, as described in Chapter 1*

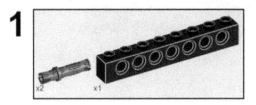

2

3

4

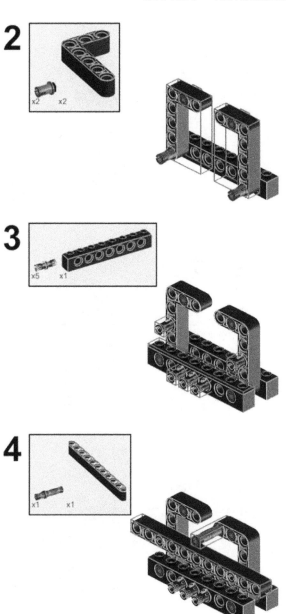

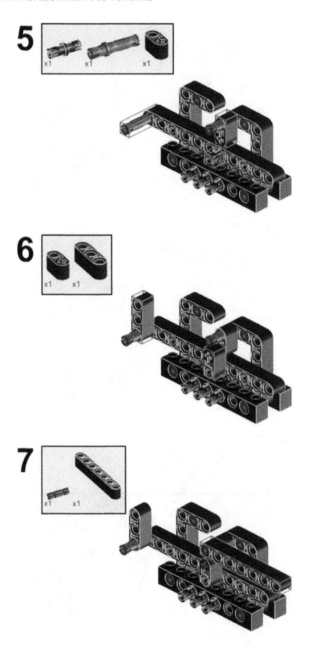

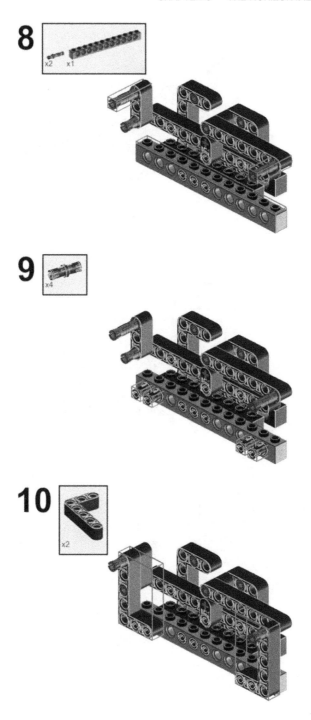

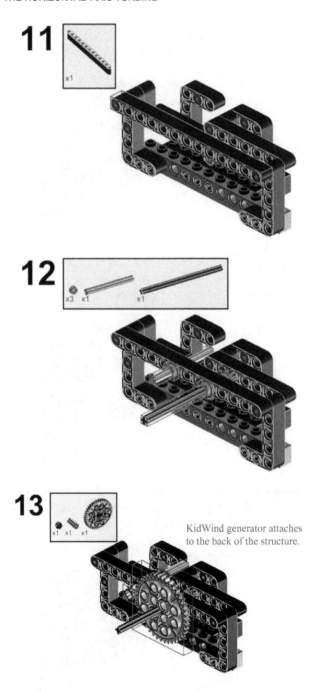

KidWind generator attaches
to the back of the structure.

Summary

This chapter has presented the construction of a horizontal-axis wind turbine, making use of the airfoil blades developed in Chapter 4. A combined generator/gearbox was built that allows the accommodation of various gear ratios. A rotor was designed to hold three airfoil blades and to fit onto an axle of the generator/gearbox. The final construction example in this chapter was an alternate generator/gearbox based on a non-LEGO generator.

CHAPTER 6

Measuring Performance

Optimizing a wind turbine's power output involves the consideration of many elements: blade pitch, blade length, number of blades, direction of rotation, gearbox ratio, and number of blades. This chapter presents a method and setup for quantifying power output, giving a measurement by which the efficacy of a design can be assessed. Incremental design changes can be quickly tested in a trial-and-error approach that converges to form the best solution.

Test Setup

A wind turbine under development can be tested with a fan, as shown in Figure 6-1. Box fans work well for this setup—a 24-inch-diameter fan is a good choice. We put the turbine about 1.5 meters away from the fan so as to allow the airflow to smooth out a bit. With the fan providing a wind source, the task becomes how to measure electrical output from the turbine. The generators described in this book produce direct current (DC) electricity, which is easy to measure with a multimeter. Multimeters are commonly available at hardware stores or online. For example, amazon. com has a suitable multimeter available for as low as $12. Our multimeter, shown in Figure 6-1, has been an old friend for over 25 years and does many types of measurements. But a simpler multimeter will suffice, needing only measurements of DC voltage and resistance.

G. Koch and E. Koch, *LEGO Wind Energy*, https://doi.org/10.1007/978-1-4842-4439-5_6

The turbine's electrical output gets connected to the multimeter, as shown in Figure 6-1, with clip leads grabbing onto the #5306 LEGO connector. Turning the turbine's rotor by hand should show a voltage indicated on the multimeter. Note the polarity of the voltage relative to which way the turbine is rotated. Clockwise rotation on the turbine will result in one voltage polarity, and counterclockwise rotation will result in the opposite polarity. The multimeter polarity should be connected so that a positive voltage is read when the turbine blades are spun in the designed direction of travel. Voltage from the turbine is somewhat useful in determining the output of the turbine as steps in optimization are being done. But what really matters from the wind turbine is output power. To measure power the turbine has to be connected to a load so the turbine can do work. The work in this case is provided by connecting a resistor to the turbine output—the resistor converts electrical energy into heat. Figure 6-2 shows how a resistor can be connected to a LEGO cable connector. A resistor is connected to the second set of points on the #5306 connector by alligator clips. In other words, the resistor and multimeter are connected in parallel. The other end of the #5306 wire, attached to nothing in Figure 6-2, would go to the #71427c01 generator.

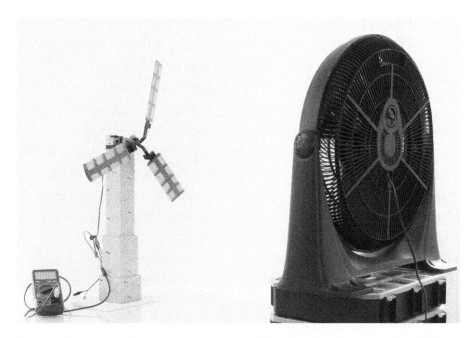

Figure 6-1. *A multimeter is connected by clip leads to a #5306 LEGO connector*

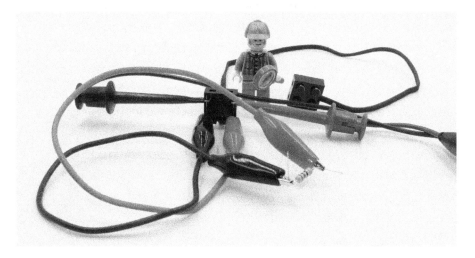

Figure 6-2. *Placing an electrical load on the turbine, while also measuring voltage, involves two sets of wires*

The choice of resistor involves two factors: resistance value and power-handling capability. Resistance, measured in ohms, is indicated on a resistor by a color code of four bands. The key to the color code can be found on the internet or is usually supplied when a kit of resistors is purchased, and we recommend buying such a kit so that various resistances can be tried. Such trial and error of resistance values is inevitable, so having a variety of resistors is convenient. In choosing the resistance it should be noted that if the resistance is too low the turbine output might be tasked with too much of a load, inhibiting the turbine rotor from even beginning to spin. On the other hand, if the resistance is too high then the turbine rotor might be allowed to spin so fast that the rotation may stall or the blades will fling off the rotor. A reasonable resistance to start with is 500 ohms, and resistance can be decreased if the rotor spins too fast.

A more complex issue arises in resistor selection in a phenomena called *impedance matching*. Impedance matching is a concept for transferring the maximum amount of electrical energy from a source to a load, which occurs when the resistance of the generator matches the resistance of the load. We found the matching condition to occur at between 400 to 500 ohms for the #71427c01 generator. For the KidWind generator the best choice of load resistance is 100 ohms. However, in the official KidWind competition the load resistance is preselected by the testing setup at 30 ohms, so there is no design choice to make regarding load resistance.

The second choice to make in specifying a resistor is its power-handling capability, measured in watts. Common power-handling specifications for resistors are 1/8, 1/4, and 1/2 watt. If the power generated by the turbine exceeds the resistor's capability, then the resistor could burn out and be destroyed. This burnout is not really spectacular nor a safety hazard, but should nonetheless be avoided. We've seen in excess of 1/4 watt from a #71427c01 LEGO generator, so a 1/2-watt resistor should be selected. In summary, for the #71427c01 LEGO generator the resistor to use is 470 ohms, 1/2 watt. Other generators will require some trial and error to find the best resistor. If a non-optimum impedance-matching resistor is used, everything will still work, but the power from the turbine won't be as high as it could be.

With the resistor selected and connected to the turbine output, power output from the turbine can be measured by noting the voltage across the resistor and calculating as follows:

power = voltage²/resistance

That is, the voltage is squared, then divided by resistance, giving turbine power output in units of watts.

LEGO-based Meter

In place of a multimeter, a LEGO-built measuring device is available in the #bb491 Energy Display, shown in Figure 6-3. The display is part of the 9688 LEGO Education Renewable Energy Add-On program for solar and wind energy. We found this add-on set as a whole to be lacking in exploring wind energy, but the Energy Display by itself is worthwhile. The Energy Display also requires the #89668 Rechargeable Battery, which will be discussed in Chapter 8. These two components are expensive at about US$110, which factors into the decision to use it versus a multimeter. The #bb491 Energy Display performs the same function as the load resistor and multimeter and automatically calculates and displays power output from the turbine. Connection to the turbine is by a Power Functions connector on the back of the meter, not shown in Figure 6-3. The Power Functions connector on the front of the meter connects to power stored within the #89668 Rechargeable Battery and will be discussed in Chapter 8. Other controls on the front panel include a green power button and an orange knob for switching the polarity when using the battery output.

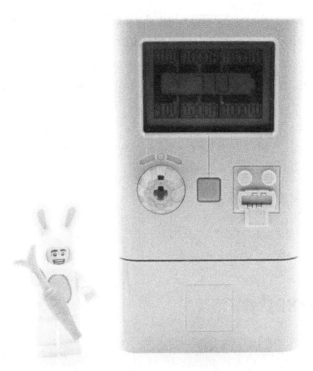

Figure 6-3. *The #bb491 Energy Display gives readings of voltage, current, and power coming into the meter*

Assessing Turbine Performance

Many factors contribute to the output power of a wind turbine, so it's useful to record power output as various options are tried. Power output can be measured with either of the two techniques described earlier in this chapter—a multimeter or the #bb491 Energy Display. Keeping a table is a good way of recording performance, with entries for turbine design parameters and the bottom-line answer for power output. An example record is shown in Table 6-1 using the turbine configuration of Figure 6-1. The result of interest is turbine output power, shown in red on the last line. If the #bb491 Energy Display is being used, the output voltage and power can simply be read off the screen. If a multimeter is connected to turbine output, power is calculated as voltage^2/resistance.

Table 6-1. *Turbine Design Parameters Are Entered into a Table And Resulting Output Measured Values of Voltage and Power Are Recorded*

Generator type	LEGO #71427c01
Blade type	26 studs long. Airfoil ribs of #50950 3x1 Curve on leading edge and #61678 4x1 Curve on trailing edge.
Blade pitch	67.5 degrees
Number of blades	3
Direction of blade rotation	Counterclockwise
Gearbox design	40:24 Technic gear ratio
Test fan orientation	Highest speed setting, 1.5 m from turbine, center of fan in line with center of turbine rotor
Load resistance	470 ohms
Measured output voltage	10.2 volts
Measured output power	**221 milliwatts**

Relationship Between Power and Energy

Power, measured in tests such as that in Table 6-1, is the rate at which energy is created with time. Sometimes the quantity of energy, rather than power, is of interest. For example, a homeowner's electric utility power bill is for energy used over the course of a month. Also, in some turbine-design competitions the amount of energy produced over a certain amount of time is the basis for judging. The KidWind competition judges the amount of energy delivered into a 30-ohm load over a 60-second period after test fans are turned on. Measuring energy is easy with the #bb491 Energy Display—it's the main number displayed on the device, shown in the unit of joules.

A manual calculation of energy, if a multimeter is being used for power measurement, involves recording power over time. If power were constant, energy could be calculated simply by multiplying power and time. But power often changes over time, such as when the test fan starts, and it takes a while for the turbine to come up to full rotation speed. Table 6-2 shows a record of power at various times after start of the test fan that will aid the calculation of energy over a 60-second time span. The power determined from the multimeter is entered into the center column at the end of the times of the first column. Energy over the intervals of time is calculated by multiplication shown and entered in the third column. The total energy is then the sum of the rows in the third column.

Table 6-2. *Calculating Energy Generated Within 60 Seconds of the Start of a Test; Includes Entering Power Measurements at Intervals Indicated in Column 1*

TIME AFTER FAN STARTS (s)	MEASURED POWER (mW)	ENERGY (mJ)
5		5 x column 2 =
10		5 x column 2 =
15		5 x column 2 =
20		5 x column 2 =
30		10 x column 2 =
40		10 x column 2 =
50		10 x column 2 =
60		10 x column 2 =
		TOTAL ENERGY = SUM OF ABOVE =

Automated Energy Measurement

The #bb491 Energy Display can interface with Mindstorms EV3, allowing computer control of energy measurement. This setup is a version of the automated test rig used at design competitions. Mindstorms hosts the #bb491 Energy Display as a sensor with software control via a programming block available at lego.com/en-us/mindstorms/download. This programming block can be seen in Figure 6-4, where an EV3 program is shown for an automated energy measurement. This algorithm also includes turning on the test fan by a device called the dSwitch, made by Dexter Industries (dexterindustries.com). The dSwitch, pictured in Figure 6-5, is a relay that takes an EV3 signal as input to turn on or off an appliance plugged into a wall outlet. The appliance in this case is the test fan.

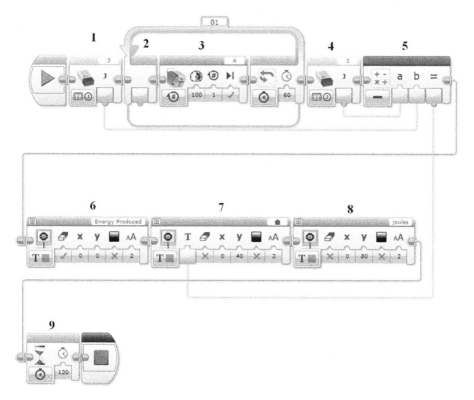

Figure 6-4. *Programming block*

Blocks in the program include the following:

1. Energy Meter Block: Reads the #bb491 Energy Display for energy stored in the #89668 Rechargeable Battery before the test begins. For the Energy Meter to function properly the stored energy before the test should be at least 1 joule. In other words, the test won't work well if the rechargeable battery is discharged. Similarly, a fully charged battery of 100 joules won't function properly in the test.

2. & 3. Loop Block: Activates the test fan via the dSwitch device for 60 seconds. The length of the test can be altered as desired. A Medium Motor block is being repurposed here to control the dSwitch.

4. Energy Meter Block: Reads the #bb491 Energy Display for energy stored in the #89668 Rechargeable Battery after the test fan has been shut down.

5. Math Block: Subtracts the initial battery charge value from the final battery charge value.

6. Display Block: Prints "Energy Produced" on the display.

7. Display Block: Indicates the value calculated in Block 5.

8. Display Block: Shows the units of energy.

9. Wait Block: Pauses the program for 120 seconds to allow the user to view the result before the program shuts down.

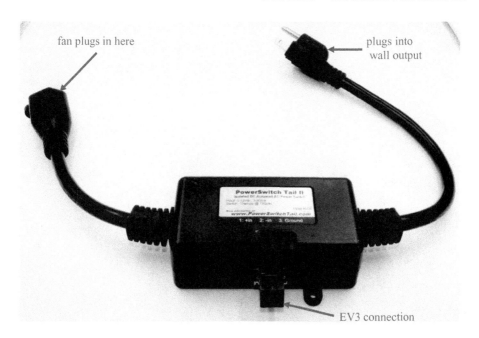

fan plugs in here

plugs into
wall output

EV3 connection

Figure 6-5. *The dSwitch can activate the test fan under Mindstorms*
EV3 control

Summary

This chapter showed how to measure the power output from a turbine
by connecting an electrical load in the form of a resistor. Guidelines were
given for selecting the specifications of the resistor. A means to measure
voltage produced by the turbine across the load resistor was described,
along with the equation for converting voltage to power. Energy, rather
than power, is sometimes the desired measurement from a turbine, so the
conversion from power to energy was shown. As an alternate to a manual
calculation of power and energy, use of the LEGO #bb491 Energy Display
was described to make automated measurements. In the next chapter, the
horizontal-axis wind turbine will be made ready for use outdoors with the
addition of a steering vane.

CHAPTER 7

Steering into the Wind

The next problem to consider for a horizontal-axis turbine is making it face into the wind direction. The fixed-direction design of Chapter 5 is fine if the direction of the wind is known so that the turbine blades can be pointed into the wind. This is the case in many wind turbine design competitions in which the wind is provided by fans. However, if using the turbine in ambient wind outdoors, the direction of the wind is unknown and variable. Hence, the turbine needs a way to steer into the wind.

The Steering Vane

A solution for steering into the wind, shown in Figure 7-1, is to attach a vane behind the rotor, along with a means to pivot the rotor. Step-by-step assembly instructions follow Figure 7-1. The large surface area of the vane gets pushed by the wind, forcing the vane to tend to be parallel to the wind. This orientation faces the blades into the wind, where rotation speed will be the highest. A video of the vane in action can be seen at hightechlego.com.

The weight of the vane should be kept to a minimum so that it is easy for the wind to push it. Hence, the vane is only one thickness of LEGO plate. A thicker vane might be stronger, but it would create more mass for the wind to push. Strength is better achieved by a few drops of Super Glue on the vane's vertical plates as they are attached to the two-stud-wide horizontal plate. The balance of the vane against the rotor blades is also of importance. Ideally, the rotating top of the turbine should not be weighed

© Grady Koch 2019
G. Koch and E. Koch, *LEGO Wind Energy*, https://doi.org/10.1007/978-1-4842-4439-5_7

down more on one side. Experiments with various vane shapes and sizes for the three-blade turbine developed in Chapter 5 resulted in the solution shown in Figure 7-1. A turbine with more blades or heavier blades may warrant a different vane design.

The top assembly of the turbine needs a way to pivot, which is accomplished with a #3403c01 Turntable. LEGO makes two kinds of turntables of this size: locking and free rotating. The type needed here is the free-rotating version so the turbine is able to turn wherever is needed with minimal resistance.

Figure 7-1. *A turntable attached between two 8x8 Bricks allows the generator/gearbox assembly to pivot*

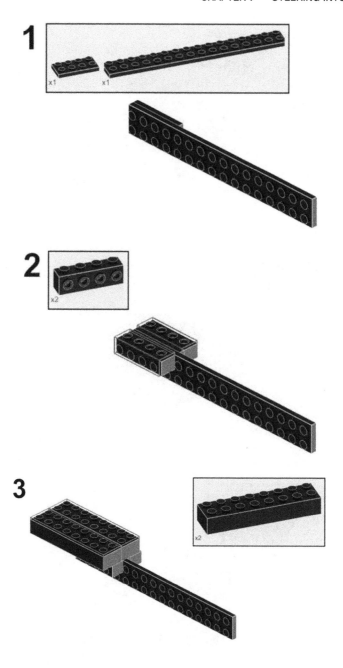

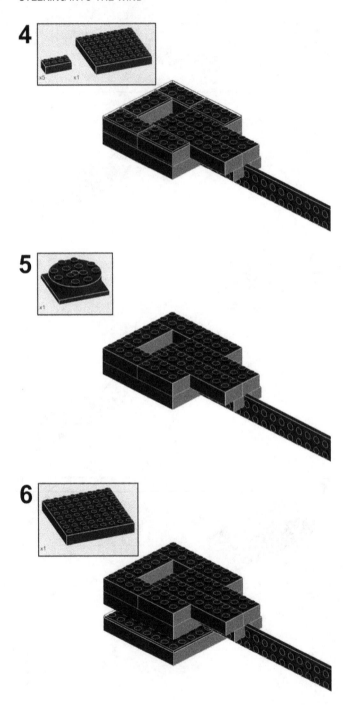

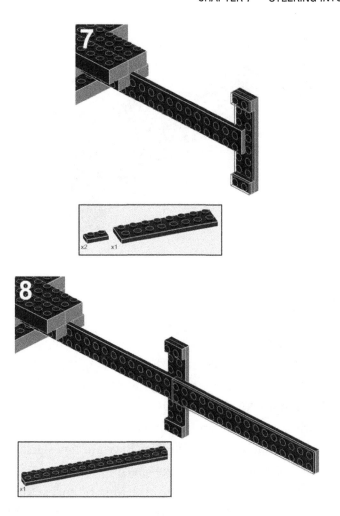

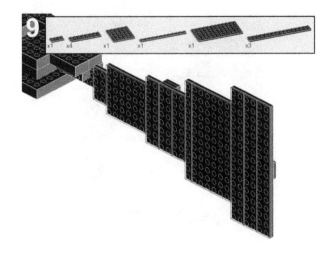

Final Assembly

Attachment to the turbine pillar is achieved by connecting the lower 8x8 Brick base of Figure 7-1 onto the 8x8 portion of the pedestal. The generator/gearbox then goes onto the upper 8x8 surface of Figure 7-1. A photo of the completed assembly is given in Figure 7-2. With the generator/gearbox now free to rotate, consideration is warranted of the electrical connector cable. This cable must have enough slack to not impede the rotation of the generator/gearbox.

A wind test outdoors can get the turbine rotating so fast that the blades or rotor parts can come loose—LEGO pieces can go flying. *Safety glasses are critical to protect oneself in such a situation.* In a way, such a situation is a positive indication that an efficient design has been built. But to keep the turbine together, we found that cyanoacrylate (such as Krazy Glue or Super Glue) is needed at key locations of blade-attachment points. We also glued the plates of the steering vane on the two-stud-wide horizontal plate.

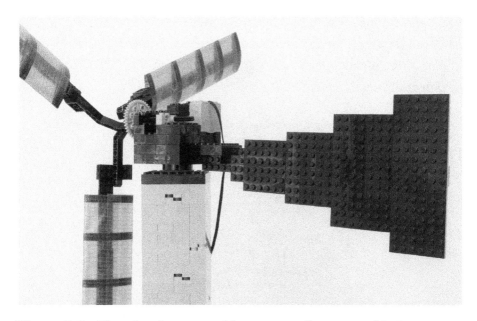

Figure 7-2. *The pivoting vane rides on top of a tower of 8x8 cross-section*

Outdoor Testing

With attachment of the steering vane, the horizontal-axis turbine is ready to go outside and generate power from the wind. We took the setup shown in Figure 7-2 to catch the breeze, as well as the vertical-axis turbine from Chapter 3. Videos of both turbines in action can be seen on the website hightechlego.com. A key feature of turbine performance is how much energy is generated over the course of many hours outdoors. The #bb491 Energy Display allows a record of energy production, and the turbine can simply be left connected to the meter to note how much energy has been stored in the #89668 Rechargeable Battery. But a more insightful assessment can be made by logging power and energy production over time, which can be recorded by interfacing the #bb491 Energy Display with Mindstorms EV3. Figure 7-3 shows a Mindstorms EV3 program for recording turbine power and energy output. This program also includes, as an option, a means to record a precise timestamp using the Dexter Industries (dexterindustries.com) dGPS sensor. Dexter Industries supplies a downloadable EV3 programming block for the dGPS, used in the program shown in Figure 7-3.

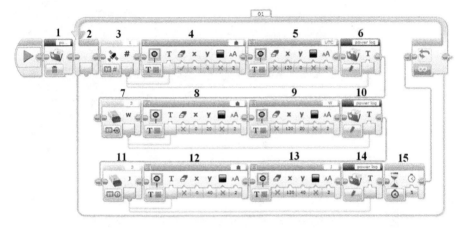

Figure 7-3. *EV3 program for recording power and energy output from a turbine includes downloaded blocks for the #bb491 Energy Display and Dexter Industries dGPS*

Blocks in the program include the following:

1. File Block: Deletes and clears data for the filename "power log".

2. Loop Block: Creates an infinite iteration of measurements. The loop is stopped when the program is manually shut down or the EV3 Intelligent Brick's battery runs out.

3. dGPS Sensor Block: Takes a reading of time for the dGPS sensor connected to Port 1. The time read is in UTC (Coordinated Universal Time), so conversion is needed if local time is preferred. This data is fed to Blocks 4 and 6.

4. Display Block: Shows time measurement on the display.

5. Display Block: Indicates the UTC label for time measurements.

6. File Block: Writes the measured time to the file "power log".

7. to 10. Performs a similar function to Blocks 3–6, but for a power measurement from the #bb491 Energy Display.

11. to 14. Performs a similar function to Blocks 3–6, but for an energy measurement from the #bb491 Energy Display.

15. Wait Block: delays the program for five seconds before running the loop again. In other words, a set of measurements is repeated every five seconds.

The result of this EV3 program is a data file called "power log" that is stored in the EV3 Intelligent Brick's memory, which can be accessed from the Memory Browser tab in the EV3 programming environment. Opening the "power log" file with a text editor will show a long column of numbers such as that seen in Figure 7-4—the first number is time, the second is turbine power, and the third is stored energy. These three numbers are repeated again every five seconds. The time measurement is recorded as an integer without the colons that separate minutes and seconds. For example, the first number in this log should be interpreted as 17:12:66. As in this example, a quirk in the GPS record is that seconds will sometimes go above 60. In other words, the example time measurement is equivalent to 17:13:06.

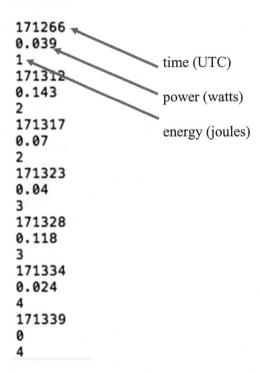

```
171266
0.039
1
171312
0.143
2
171317
0.07
2
171323
0.04
3
171328
0.118
3
171334
0.024
4
171339
0
4
```

time (UTC)

power (watts)

energy (joules)

Figure 7-4. *Example of "power log" data file created by the EV3 program in Figure 7-3*

The numbers in Figure 7-4 can be separated and collected in columns of a spreadsheet to then be plotted. Such a plot is given in Figure 7-5, with blue circles indicating power and red squares indicating stored energy. The #89668 Rechargeable Battery has a capacity of 100 joules, so the #bb491 Energy Display shuts off input when 100 joules has been reached. Hence, the measurement of Figure 7-5 was run until 100 joules was reached. It took about one hour of wind-power generation to reach the 100-joule mark. The time required to fully charge depends, of course, on wind speed. The wind conditions during the test were not very strong, with wind speed ranging between zero and 4 m/s. The area in which we live in coastal Virginia typically has a low wind speed, being a low elevation thickly populated with tall trees. The wind of Figure 7-5 came in occasional bursts, with gusts picking up after the first third of the experiment.

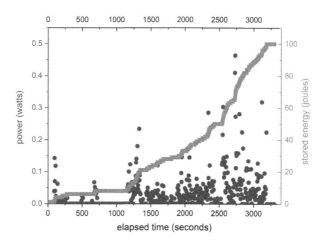

Figure 7-5. *Results of an outdoor wind-power test are plotted with automated logging of power and energy produced by the turbine*

Summary

This chapter added a steering vane to a horizontal-axis wind turbine, enabling the turbine to keep its blades pointed into the wind. The vane works by creating a large, lightweight surface area behind the blades such that the vane aligns itself with oncoming wind. With the addition of the vane the turbine can effectively be used outdoors in an environment where the wind direction is variable. A test setup was developed to measure the performance of outdoor power generation, with automated recording of turbine output power and energy. In the next chapter, ideas will be introduced for using the energy produced by a LEGO wind turbine.

CHAPTER 8

Powering Things

Once turbines are spinning and generating electricity, attention can be turned to what to do with this power. Designs are shown here for powering circuits or LEGO motors from wind energy. The power from a turbine generator can be of varying voltage, so solutions are presented in this chapter to regulate voltage or store charge in a battery.

LEDs Powered by Wind

We've always been amused by making things light up, with light emitting diodes (LEDs) a favorite subject. So, we built a circuit to power LEDs from the turbine output. This light display adds to the visual appeal of the turbine, combining the eye-catching spinning of the rotor with flashing colors. It's the ultimate kinetic garden sculpture.

© Grady Koch 2019
G. Koch and E. Koch, *LEGO Wind Energy*, https://doi.org/10.1007/978-1-4842-4439-5_8

Figure 8-1. *Two LED package styles to consider are the 3 mm, held by the dancer, and 5 mm, at her feet*

LEDs are available in many colors, brightnesses, and package sizes. The package sizes of 3 mm or 5 mm offer variety, are low cost, and are easy to insert into circuits. The package size refers to the diameter of the LED's base. For the tinkering-minded person, an assortment of both of these package shapes in several colors can be inexpensively purchased in parts kits, such as part number 2238338 from jameco.com. Figure 8-1 shows our favorite LED design that automatically cycles through colors. The wire leads on an LED are rather long and can be trimmed to a desired length with wire cutters. However, before trimming the leads it's important to remember which lead is longer—this is the positive connection. Another mark of polarity is on the base of the LED, with the base squared off near the negative polarity lead. The positive lead of the LED has to be connected to positive voltage; getting the polarity reversed can destroy the LED. An LED often needs a resistor in front of it to limit the current consumed by the LED. An excellent tutorial and calculator for choosing the values of the resistor can be found at ledcalc.com. A circuit for powering the LED is shown in the schematic in Figure 8-2 and in practice in Figure 8-4. This circuit is built onto a breadboard, a platform for making the wire connections between electronics components. Instructions for using a breadboard can be found on the internet, and many electronics retailers have online instructions. We used double-sided tape to attach the breadboard to a #64179 Open Center Liftarm so that the breadboard can be installed at the base of the turbine.

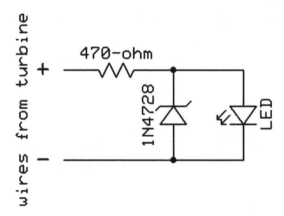

Figure 8-2. *A circuit for powering an LED from turbine output includes a current-limiting resistor and a 1N4728 Zener diode acting as a voltage regulator*

Figure 8-3. *The Zener diode has a black band at one end to represent the cathode*

A complication of using the turbine output is that the voltage varies as the wind changes speed. Converting this variable DC voltage to a constant usable voltage can be accomplished with a Zener diode, which acts as a voltage regulator. The Zener diode, pictured in Figure 8-3, is a model 1N4728 and provides an output of 3.3 volts for whatever voltage is coming from the turbine, as long as turbine voltage is higher than 3.3 volts. Zener diodes have a polarity for their connection, indicated by a black ring around the end called a *cathode*. The cathode is connected to positive voltage for a Zener diode in a configuration called *reverse bias*. The Zener diode requires an input of greater than 3.3 volts, so if the turbine is not turning fast enough to produce more than 3.3 volts, the LED will not light up. A more effective design, described in the following section, is to store energy from the turbine to parse out energy when the wind is not blowing.

Figure 8-4. *The circuit of Figure 8-2 can be implemented as a breadboard circuit, with the red and black wires connected to the turbine by alligator clips as shown in Figure 6-2*

Charging a Battery

A useful design for powering things from a turbine is to use the turbine's output to charge a battery. The #89668 Rechargeable Battery device provides a convenient way to do this. The energy meter that mates with the #89668 Rechargeable Battery was used in Chapters 6 and 7, and now the full capability is used. The easiest way to tap energy from the #89668 Rechargeable Battery is to connect Power Functions devices to the front panel of the #bb491 Energy Display. Figure 8-5 shows such a connection with a motorized device powered by energy stored from the wind. The Power Functions device shown here is an intermittent motion demonstration inspired by Yoshihito Isogawa's design in his *The LEGO*

Mindstorms EV3 Idea Book. Power drained from the battery is measured at the bottom part of the #bb491 Energy Display, so the power consumed by the load is quantified. Of course, energy can also be added to the system if the turbine is rotating.

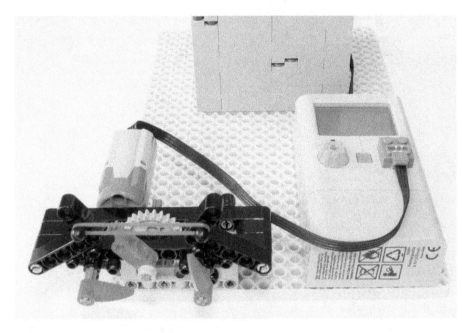

Figure 8-5. *The combined #bb491 Energy Display and #89668 Rechargeable Battery, charged up by wind energy, is connected to a Power Functions construction*

For a more basic design using discrete electronic components, the battery output from the #89668 Rechargeable Battery can also be used to power breadboard circuits. For example, color-changing LEDs can be run by the battery output. A circuit to do so is shown in schematic form in Figure 8-6 and as an implementation in Figure 8-7. Voltage is regulated by the #bb491 Energy Display, so an element to regulate voltage is not needed, as was used in connection direct from the turbine of Figure 8-2. A current-limiting resistor provides protection for the LEDs, with a ¼-watt resistor sufficient for power handling. A higher-rated power resistor is also satisfactory—higher-rated powers are always acceptable. Three LEDs are used here for an interesting display. For example, different-color LEDs can be selected. If fewer LEDs are used, then the resistor's value should be increased (ledcalc.com can be used to select the resistor).

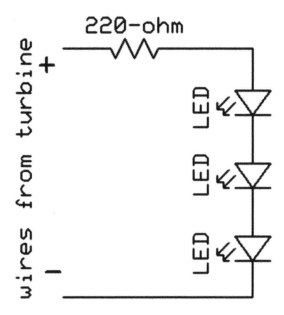

Figure 8-6. *The schematic for driving LEDs involves a resistor in series with the LEDs*

Summary

This chapter explored ways to use the energy created by a wind turbine, including driving light emitting diodes or LEGO motors. Power directly from a turbine can be put to use but is intermittent as wind comes and goes. A more effective design is to use a turbine to charge a battery, with an example given of charging the battery associated with the #bb491 Energy Display. In the next chapter, the first example of an advanced turbine design is presented.

Figure 8-7. *The same breadboard-on-a-liftarm of Figure 8-4 is used again here to implement the schematic from Figure 8-6*

CHAPTER 9

A Dual-Rotor Turbine

In this chapter an idea is explored of placing two rotors on a single pillar. In our experiments adding another set of blades to a horizontal-axis turbine, such as that in Figure 5-1, did not improve power output. The extra weight of the second set of blades overcame any added rotation speed. However, adding another generator on the same pillar can provide more power.

Counter-Rotating Blades

Figure 9-1 shows the dual-rotor, dual-generator design. The blades are arranged to counter-rotate to avoid problems in balancing the pillar when the blades are spinning. Counter-rotation means that when viewed from one side of the turbine, one set of blades is going counterclockwise and the other set is going clockwise. This counter-rotation is appealing to watch—videos can be found on hightechlego.com. The same pedestal was used for the other turbines built in earlier chapters. Blades have been used of the same design used for the horizontal-axis turbine in Chapter 5, except a set has been made for clockwise rotation. The counterclockwise blade set is in blue tape, while the clockwise set is in clear tape. Figure 9-2, and instructions following the figure, provides the design for the dual-generator configuration. Mindstorms' dual-bevel gears are used here for the gearbox for a change of pace from the Technic gears used in earlier chapters.

© Grady Koch 2019
G. Koch and E. Koch, *LEGO Wind Energy*, https://doi.org/10.1007/978-1-4842-4439-5_9

Figure 9-1. The dual-rotor turbine features two generators on one pedestal

Figure 9-2. The dual-generator design has two #71427c01 generators facing opposite directions

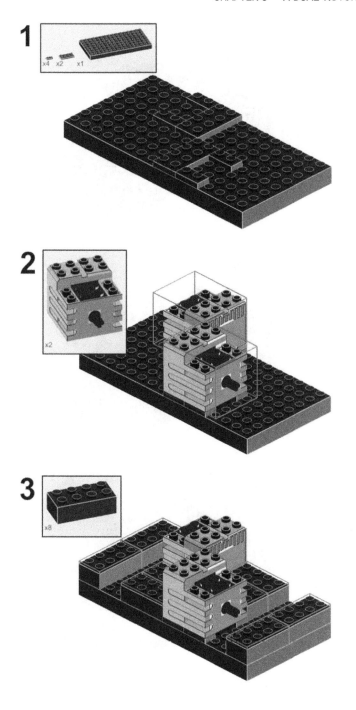

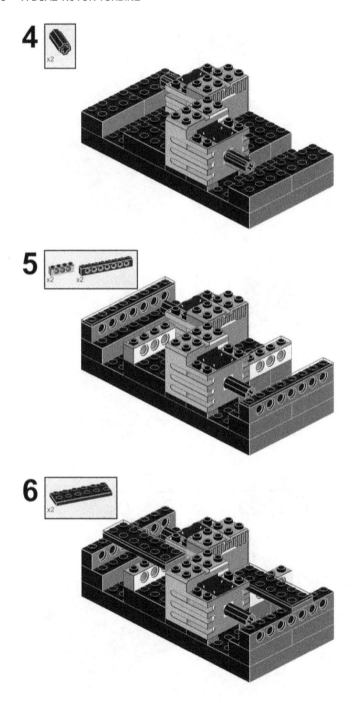

7

8

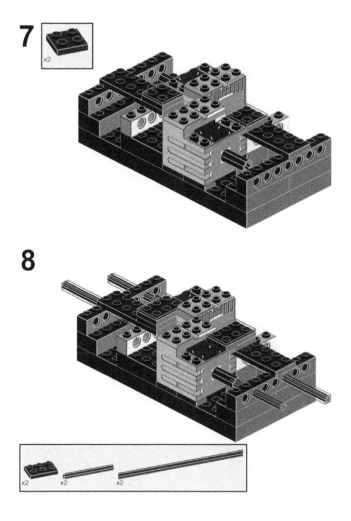

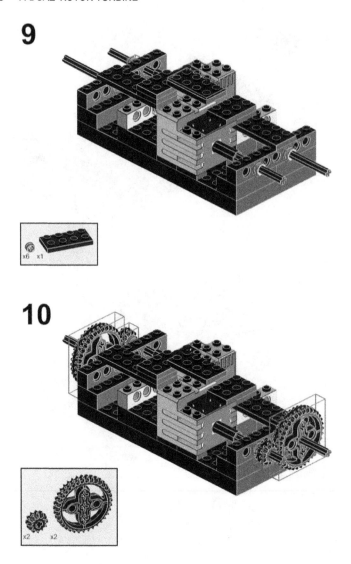

Electrical Connection

Each of the generators needs a connection by a #5306 Wire, and each of these two connectors could go to separate storage batteries. But the connection can also be made in a parallel circuit by snapping the #5306 connectors on top of each other, as shown in Figure 9-3. This combined connector can then be fed to a single rechargeable battery, as was done in Chapter 8 with connection to the #89668 Rechargeable Battery. The power coming out of the dual-rotor turbine is almost twice that of a conventional single-rotor design. It's not a doubling of power, as might be expected, because there is some loss in the dual-rotor design for two reasons: (1) the front rotor steals some of the wind strength from the rotor behind it, and (2) the parallel electrical connection involves some power from one generator being sent to the second generator and vice versa. The second point of the generators' electrically interacting with each other can be seen by turning off the test fan and manually turning one rotor—the other rotor will rotate.

Figure 9-3. *Cables from the two generators can be connected in parallel by stacking #5306 wire connectors*

Summary

This chapter attached two rotors, along with two generators, to a single pillar. The two rotors were made to rotate in opposite directions to balance the forces applied to the pillar when the rotors are spinning. With two generators producing electricity, the electrical power is almost double that of a conventional single-rotor turbine. The power from the two generators can be combined in parallel to charge a battery. In the next chapter, another advanced turbine design will be explored by using pneumatic pressure generation rather than electrical generation.

CHAPTER 10

A Pneumatic Generator

The turbines built in earlier chapters, and indeed almost all turbines, are based on producing electrical energy. But energy can also be produced and stored in the form of compressed air. This pneumatic generator involves using the rotating shaft of the turbine rotor to drive an air pump. Instead of a battery, energy from the turbine is stored in an air tank.

Design of the Pneumatic Turbine

The pneumatic turbine shown in Figure 10-1 features the same blades, rotor, and pedestal used in earlier chapters. But the generator is an entirely different design, based on #19482c01 Pneumatic Pump. Rotary motion from the spinning blades is converted to a linear drive for the air pump by a mechanism called an *eccentric*. A close-up of the generator is presented in Figure 10-2, and step-by-step assembly instructions follow the figure. A gearbox was found not to be needed, since the spinning rotor gave enough speed to operate the air pump. Air compressed by the pump is fed into a storage tank attached to the back of the generator structure.

© Grady Koch 2019
G. Koch and E. Koch, *LEGO Wind Energy*, https://doi.org/10.1007/978-1-4842-4439-5_10

Figure 10-1. *The pneumatic generator uses a pump to compress air into a storage tank*

Figure 10-2. *The pneumatic generator is based on a #19482c01 Pneumatic Pump, in blue in this image*

1

2

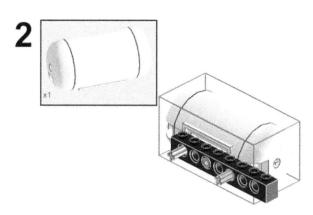

3

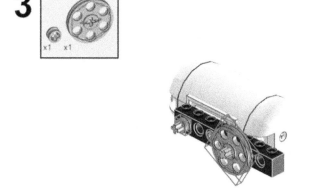

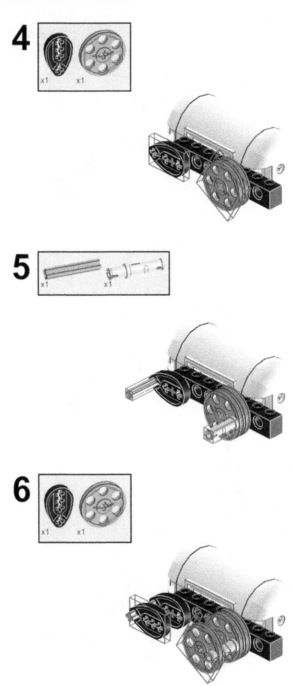

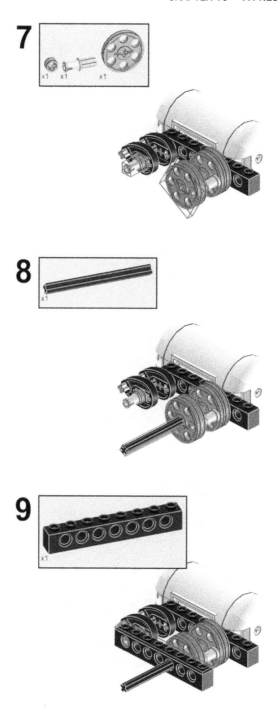

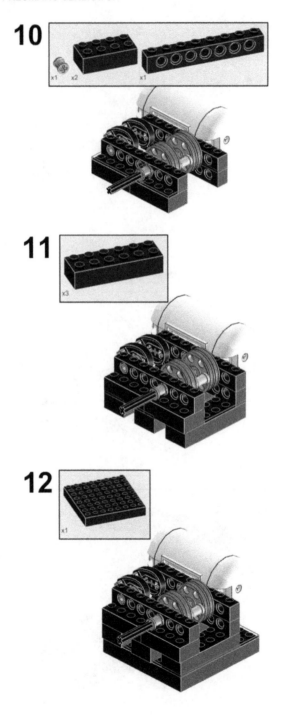

Pneumatic Connection

As shown in Figure 10-1, air from the #19482c01 Pneumatic Pump moves via a pneumatic hose to one side of the air tank. The other connection to the air tank goes to useful output, connected to whatever pneumatic work is to be done. Compressed air stored in the air tank can be periodically released to power various pneumatic devices by a pneumatic switch, as implemented in Figure 10-3. A pneumatic hose joins the output of the air tank to a pneumatic switch. Useful output, not connected in the case of Figure 10-3, is on one side of the switch. Both the switch and a manometer are held by a #3702 1x8 Technic Brick. This brick is attached to the pedestal. The other side of the switch, connected to a manometer for measuring air pressure, is engaged with pressure building up inside the tank. We found that as pressure builds up inside the tank the rotor encounters more resistance and slows down.

Figure 10-3. *An air line is connected from the air tank to the center port on a pneumatic switch*

Summary

Most wind turbines use electrical generators to create power, but this chapter showed that power can also be generated and stored in the form of compressed air. In this pneumatic turbine, the spinning blades turn a mechanism to operate an air pump. The design for an eccentric was shown to convert rotary motion to linear motion to drive a pneumatic pump. Compressed air is stored in an air tank, with a design given to monitor stored air pressure and to release pressure for driving pneumatic devices.

APPENDIX

Parts Lists

This appendix provides parts lists for the constructions found throughout this book, with a table summarizing LEGO parts used in each set of building instructions. Part numbers are identified so that they may be quickly found at seller sites, such as bricklink.com.

Table A-1. *Parts list for Chapter 1: Putting a Generator to Use*

Quantity	Item Number	Description
1	71427c01	9V Electric Motor
1	3020	2x4 Plate
2	3023	1x2 Plate
2	32028	1x2 Plate with Door Rail
2	3703	1x16 Technic Brick with Holes
1	2780	Technic Pin with Friction Ridges
3	87079	2x4 Tile
1	6538c	Technic Axle Connector
1	2420	2x2 Corner Plate
1	32062	Technic Axle 2 Notched
1	32348	1x7 Bent Liftarm
1	4771	1x4 Electric Light Brick
1	32556	Long Technic Pin without Friction Ridges

© Grady Koch 2019
G. Koch and E. Koch, *LEGO Wind Energy*, https://doi.org/10.1007/978-1-4842-4439-5

Table A-2. *Parts list for Chapter 2: Gearing Up*

Quantity	Item Number	Description
1	71427c01	9V Electric Motor
1	3020	2x4 Plate
2	3023	1x2 Plate
2	32028	1x2 Plate with Door Rail
2	3703	1x16 Technic Brick with Holes
1	2780	Technic Pin with Friction Ridges
3	87079	2x4 Tile
1	2420	2x2 Corner Plate
1	4771	1x4 Electric Light Brick
1	3648	24 Tooth Technic Gear
1	4265c	Technic Bush 1/2
1	3649	40 Tooth Technic Gear
1	6538c	Technic Axle Connector
1	32062	Technic Axle 2 Notched
1	32348	1x7 Bent Liftarm
1	32556	Long Technic Pin without Friction Ridges
1	32209	Technic Axle 5.5 with Stop

Table A-3. *Parts list for Chapter 2: Compound Gears*

Quantity	Item Number	Description
1	71427c01	9V Electric Motor
1	3020	2x4 Plate
2	3023	1x2 Plate
2	32028	1x2 Plate with Door Rail
2	3703	1x16 Technic Brick with Holes
1	2780	Technic Pin with Friction Ridges
3	87079	2x4 Tile
1	2420	2x2 Corner Plate
1	4771	1x4 Electric Light Brick
2	3648	24 Tooth Technic Gear
1	3706	Technic Axle 6
2	3649	40 Tooth Technic Gear
3	4265c	Technic Bush 1/2
1	32209	Technic Axle 5.5 with Stop
1	6538c	Technic Axle Connector
1	32062	Technic Axle 2 Notched
1	32556	Long Technic Pin without Friction Ridges
1	32348	1x7 Bent Liftarm

Table A-4. *Parts list for Chapter 3: Generator Mount*

Quantity	Item Number	Description
1	71427c01	9V Electric Motor
2	3701	1x4 Technic Brick with Holes
2	3700	1x2 Technic Brick with Holes
4	6558	Long Technic Pin with Friction Ridges
2	3894	1x6 Technic Brick with Holes
2	32017	1x5 Thin Technic Liftarm
2	32524	1x7 Technic Liftarm
2	48989	Technic 4 Pin Connector
4	2456	2x6 Brick
1	6538c	Technic Axle Connector
2	3795	2x6 Plate
1	4201	8x8 Brick

Table A-5. *Parts list for Chapter 3: Gearbox Frame*

Quantity	Item Number	Description
1	64178	5x11 Open Center Frame Liftarm
22	2780	Technic Pin with Friction Ridges
6	32523	1x3 Technic Liftarm
1	41239	1x13 Technic Liftarm
2	32524	1x7 Technic Liftarm
4	41678	Axle and Pin Connector Perpendicular Double Split
4	32062	Technic Axle 2 Notched
3	32525	1x11 Technic Liftarm
2	6558	Long Technic Pin with Friction Ridges
2	48989	Technic 4 Pin Connector
1	55013	Technic Axle 8 with Stop
1	4265c	Technic Bush 1/2
1	3648	24 Tooth Technic Gear

Table A-6. *Parts list for Chapter 3: The Rotor. Table describes one rotor--a multiple stack of rotors would involve multiplying quantities by the number of rotor stacks.*

Quantity	Item Number	Description
1	57585	Technic Axle Connector Hub
3	32009	1x11.5 Double Bent Liftarm
3	43093	Technic Axle Pin with Friction Ridges
6	2780	Technic Pin with Friction Ridges
3	32278	1x15 Technic Liftarm
6	3794	1x2 Jumper Plate
3	98107	11x11 Cylinder Hemisphere

Table A-7. *Parts list for Chapter 3: Mount for KidWind Generator*

Quantity	Item Number	Description
1	4204	8x16 Brick
2	3007	2x8 Brick
2	3702	1x8 Technic Brick with Holes
8	2780	Technic Pin with Friction Ridges
2	64179	5x7 Open Center Frame Liftarm
2	32140	2x4 L-Shape Liftarm
4	32054	Long Technic Pin with Friction Ridges and Stop Bush
2	32002	Tech Pin 3/4
1	32065	1x7 Thin Technic Liftarm
2	43093	Technic Axle Pin with Friction Ridges
3	32524	1x7 Technic Liftarm
4	6558	Long Technic Pin with Friction Ridges

Table A-8. *Parts list for Chapter 4: The Airfoil. This Table describes construction of one blade--multiple blades would involve multiplying quantities by the number of blades.*

Quantity	Item Number	Description
1	4282	2x16 Plate
1	3832	2x10 Plate
1	4477	1x10 Plate
8	3024	1x1 Plate
5	50950	3x1 Curved Slope
5	61678	4x1 Curved Slope

Table A-9. *Parts list for Chapter 5: The Generator/Gearbox*

Quantity	Item Number	Description
1	4201	8x8 Brick
2	3023	1x2 Plate
1	3020	2x4 Plate
1	71427c	9V Electric Motor
4	3001	2x4 Brick
1	6538c	Technic Axle Connector
1	3702	1x8 Technic Brick with Holes
1	3701	1x4 Technic Brick with Holes
1	3708	Technic Axle 12
1	32073	Technic Axle 5
3	4265c	Technic Bush 1/2
1	3795	2x6 Plate
2	3022	2x2 Plate
1	3021	2x3 Plate
1	3648	24 Tooth Technic Gear
1	3649	40 Tooth Technic Gear

Table A-10. *Parts list for Chapter 5: Rotor and Blade Attachment*

Quantity	Item Number	Description
1	57585	Technic Axle Connector Hub
3	32009	1x11.5 Double Bent Liftarm
6	44301	1x2 Locking Hinge Plate with Finger on End
6	44302	1x2 Locking Hinge Plate with Two Fibers on End
6	3022	2x2 Plate

Table A-11. *Parts list for Chapter 5: Mount for KidWind Generator*

Quantity	Item Number	Description
2	3702	1x8 Technic Brick with Holes
6	6558	Long Technic Pin with Friction Ridges
4	32526	3x5 L-Shape Liftarm
2	4274	Technic Pin 1/2
10	2780	Technic Pin with Friction Ridges
1	32525	1x11 Technic Liftarm
2	60483	1x2 Liftarm with Pin Hole and Axle Hole
1	32523	1x3 Technic Liftarm
1	32062	Technic Axle 2 Notched
1	32524	1x7 Technic Liftarm
1	3895	1x12 Technic Brick with Holes
1	41239	1x13 Technic Liftarm
1	3707	Technic Axle 8
1	32073	Technic Axle 5
3	4265c	Technic Bush 1/2
1	3649	40 Tooth Technic Gear
1	6538c	Technic Axle Connector
1	3647	8 Tooth Technic Gear

Table A-12. *Parts list for Chapter 7: The Steering Vane*

Quantity	Item Number	Description
5	4282	2x16 Plate
2	3020	2x4 Plate
2	30414	1x4 Brick with 4 Studs on Side
2	3007	2x8 Brick
2	4201	8x8 Brick
5	3001	2x4 Brick
1	3403c01	4x4 Turntable
5	3034	2x8 Plate
2	3023	1x2 Plate
1	3028	6x12 Plate
1	60479	1x12 Plate
1	3958	6x6 Plate

Table A-13. *Parts list for Chapter 9: Counter-Rotating Blades*

Quantity	Item Number	Description
2	32073	Technic Axle 5
6	4265c	Technic Bush 1/2
2	32270	12 Tooth Double Bevel Gear
2	32498	36 Tooth Double Bevel Gear
2	71427c01	9V Electric Motor
8	3001	2x4 Brick
2	6538c	Technic Axle Connector
2	3702	1x8 Technic Brick with Holes
2	3701	1x4 Technic Brick with Holes
2	3795	2x6 Plate
2	3022	2x2 Plate
2	3021	2x3 Plate
2	3708	Technic Axle 12
3	3020	2x4 Plate
4	3023	1x2 Plate
1	4204	8x16 Brick

Table A-14. *Parts list for Chapter 10: Design of the Pneumatic Turbine*

Quantity	Item Number	Description
3	3702	1x8 Technic Brick with Holes
2	4519	Technic Axle 3
3	3749	Technic Axle Pin without Friction Ridges
1	67c01	Pneumatic Airtank
2	4265c	Technic Bush 1/2
4	4185	Technic Wedge Belt Wheel
2	6575	Technic Cam
1	32556	Long Technic Pin without Friction Ridges
1	19482c01	Pneumatic Pump
1	3706	Technic Axle 6
2	3001	2x4 Brick
1	3713	Technic Bush
3	2456	2x6 Brick
1	4201	8x8 Brick

Index

CPSIA information can be obtained
at www.ICGtesting.com   .
Printed in the USA
BVHW040216180419
545888BV00009B/140/P

9 781484 244388